Journal Of Travels From St. Josephs To Oregon

by

Riley Root

Journal Of Travels From St. Josephs To Oregon

by Riley Root

ISBN: 978-93-62768-01-8

Published by

DOUBLE 9 BOOKS

2/13-B, Ansari Road
Daryaganj, New Delhi – 110002
info@double9books.com
www.double9books.com
Tel. 011-40042856

ABOUT THE AUTHOR

Riley Root, a seasoned adventurer and storyteller, unveils the epic journey chronicled in his masterpiece "Journal of Travels From St. Josephs to Oregon." Through vivid prose and keen observation, Root invites readers to embark on a compelling odyssey across the untamed landscapes of the American West. From the rugged trails of the Oregon Trail to the breathtaking vistas of the Rocky Mountains, Root's journal captures the essence of frontier life in the 19th century with remarkable detail and authenticity. As he traverses vast plains, navigates treacherous rivers, and encounters diverse cultures along the way, Root's narrative unfolds as a testament to the resilience of the human spirit and the spirit of exploration that defined an era. "Journal of Travels From St. Josephs to Oregon" stands as a timeless tribute to the pioneers who braved the unknown in search of opportunity, adventure, and a new beginning amidst the vast expanse of the American wilderness.

CONTENTS

CHAPTER I

Journey from home—Trip down the Mississippi and up the
Missouri River to St. Josephs.

I left home in Knox county, Illinois, the 3d day of April, 1848, for
Woodstock in Fulton county, a distance of about 20 miles, where I staid
one day with my eldest daughter. I then started for the Mississippi river, to
Nauvoo, a Mormon town, by the way of La Harp, a distance of fifty miles,
over which route most of the way to La Harp is as handsome prairie as I
have seen in the State. I visited the Temple at Nauvoo, with the expectation
of seeing a beautiful edifice, as the Mormons would have it to appear, that
the glory of the latter Temple is to exceed that of the former.

It is true that on approaching the Temple[1] the visitor beholds something
exquisite in its outward appearance, though not more so than many other
buildings in America, but on visiting its inner scenery, the visitor is not
arousd by any thing sublime, curious or tasteful. The inner arrangements
may be in accordance with their plans of order and church government,
yet the design and workmanship are of an ordinary appearance. But the
building is fast going to decay, and the town is vacated of three fourths of
its inhabitants.

[1] It has since been burnt.

From this place I passd down the river to Quincy, where I stopd with
a design to visit my youngest daughter of sixteen years of age, who is
attending school at the Mission Institute, about two miles east of Quincy.
The school at this place was establishd for the purpose of promoting the
cause of Christ by preparing youth for the missionary field, though other
scholars who do not wish to enter upon missionary labors are sometimes
admitted.

From Quincy I went to St. Louis for the purpose of obtaining a boat to
go to St. Josephs on the Missouri river, where most of the emigrants meet
before leaving the United States for Oregon. On ascending the Missouri
river from its confluence with the Mississippi to Weston, a town twenty-five
miles by land below St. Josephs, no pleasant villages are seen except Jefferson
City, the capital of the State of Missouri. This town shows something of the

beauties of art, with a good levee for the lading and unlading of goods. The state house is worthy of the most notice of the traveler. It is large and elegant, and made of hewn stone.

To the geologist the Missouri river presents a scene of speculation. Its waters are always muddy, and still more so at high stages of the river. To the indifferent observer it may appear that the raw edges of its banks, by their crumbling off at times of high water, furnish material for its turbid appearance at all times. It is true that in times of high water its muddy look is greatly increased, but this is not all that is to be considered. The river has but small depth of water most of the time, and this passes over an argilaceous bottom, with sufficient force to keep it constantly agitated. There is also a mixture of exceedingly fine sand spread over its bottom, and the whole together is constantly agitated by the motion of its waters. The bed of the stream from its union with the Mississippi to St. Josephs, is at least one hundred feet below the high prairie of the country around it. The question naturally arises as to the length of time required to excavate such a channel through a country so vast in extent as the Missouri traverses with all its tributaries, considering the amount of alluvium carried outward into the ocean from age to age, whilst the bed of the river is supplied in part from the high countries of its tributaries, and thus rendering the work of degradation exceedingly slow. Yet notwithstanding the amount of soil received from year to year from above, that river carries outward into the ocean more than it receives, and thereby causes a lowering of its bed, though not visible for ages, yet gradually and slowly has it worn away the earth to its present condition. The geologist has no certain means of ascertaining with certainty the amount of degradation from year to year, and must leave the subject, sublime as it is, to the wild fancies of imagination.

CHAPTER II

St. Josephs—The Indian country lying west of the River—
Formation of the Prairie—Scouring material of the Soil—Its
general appearance as far west as the South Pass, or dividing
ridge.

St. Josephs is a new town on the Missouri river, in latitude of about 34 deg. 45 min. north, with about 1800 inhabitants, which five years ago was a field of hemp. The town has 18 stores, 3 drug stores, 9 groceries, 6 tailor shops, 8 blacksmith shops, 2 tin shops, 3 taverns, 3 boarding houses, 1 steam and 1 water flouring mill, and 2 steam saw mills. Among its inhabitants are 15 lawyers, 11 doctors, 2 silversmiths and 2 gunsmiths.

The town is mostly located on a plat of ground with sufficient descent for drainage, contiguous to the bluffs on the north, on which it is partly built. On this bluff stands the court house of Buchanan county, where the spectator can overlook the town.

The river from this point is seen but a short distance either up or down, in consequence of its meandering course, so that it is soon lost sight of behind the bluffs.

I left St. Josephs for the Indian country lying west of the Missouri river, through which I was to pass on my way to Oregon, with a train of emigrants for that place, on the 25th of April, 1848, with a view of reaching Oregon before the inclemencies of winter should overtake me, under as favorable auspices as the nature of the case would allow.

The Indian country is a wild, uncultivated tract, and almost destitute of inhabitants. It has, however, a few scattering tribes of Indians, though few indeed and far between. This country is what is calld a prairie country or natural meadow, with very little timber except along the water-courses. It is a continuation of the great valley of the Mississippi westward along the tributaries to the Rocky mountains, where the waters of the continent divide and run westward into the Pacific ocean.

A prairie may be an alluvial country, and it may be tertiary. The one here spoken of is alluvial. At a remote period, the timber and loose material of the country, as well as all prairie districts, were fired by its inhabitants or by lightning, and this continued for ages will destroy the timber and leave its soil to be clothd only by the grasses, an inferior but oftentimes resplendent robe.

The traveler soon after leaving St. Josephs, westward sees prairie in all stages of formation, from the dense forest to an entire prairie. This, with the dense forests of young timber eastward, where the white man has forbidden the practice of firing prairies, seems to be a convincing proof of the aforementioned mode of prairie formation.

It has been noticed in the State of Illinois, and some other places, where the plowman is permitted to glide his plow smoothly over the beautiful landscape, that there is an exceedingly fine scouring material lying near the surface of the soil, so that steel mold boards, on a very short use of them, are seen to present a polishd surface, on drawing them from the soil. — Ages of constant burning of the prairie grasses must necessarily produce a great amount of very fine coal dust and ashes, which, by the beating rains from year to year, would cause it to mingle with the earth to the depth of several inches. Such is the probable cause of the scouring material of these plains.

On passing over the country from St. Josephs to the dividing ridge of the continent, along the emigrant route to Oregon, the traveler accustomd only to fertile districts, is greatly surprised at finding so great a portion of the continent an almost barren waste. From St. Josephs to the Platt river, a distance of 250 miles, is most of the way a country of soil and fertility.

On arriving at the Platt river, a beautifully flat country presents itself, where nature, it would seem, has but an easy task to burden the ground with excessive vegetation, but behold a country of extensive bottom lands, of feeble soil much of the way, and still more feeble at the distance, among the bluffs and rolling country.

Soon after our arrival at Platt, one day while sitting on its banks watching our cattle, I could but reflect on the situation of the country, the emigrant and his journey to Oregon, which I have here expressd in the following form.

> One evening at twilight, whilst sitting to view,
>
> On the banks of the Platt, to me 'twas quite new,
>
> Nor sadden or lonely, as one in despair
>
> Sees the beasts of the forest just 'mergd from their lair,
>
> But cheerful and tranquil, I cast my eyes o'er
>
> The wide-spreading Platt, where I ne'er roamd before.
>
> Its banks are all plat, and its islands are flat,

Its waters are tranquil, and turbid at that.

Protrusion of sandbars are seen all along,

To hinder the boatman—here's nought of his song.

Still anxious for knowledge, I turnd me around.

And saw at short distance what coverd the ground.

'Twere wagons, full many, an Oregon train,

Who'd left their lovd homes, ne'er to see them again.

If you ask what their hearts speak whilst moving along,

I fear they will mingle a tear with their song,

Whilst telling the story of wandering so far,

With their dear earthly all in their pockets and car.

The parent is anxious for his loving child,

The dame is more careless, less cautious and mild,

The lad cares for little, if father is near,

Of wars or of bloodshed—he'll shrink to the rear.

Then who shall watch over, and daily provide

For this onward band, which so near are allid?

'Tis He who makes water spring out of the rock,

Abundance shall follow—He cares for His flock.

Then onward, brave pilgrims, your Canaan is near,

You'll soon cross the Jordan [cascades] with hearts full of cheer.

On advancing up the Platt a distance of about 445 miles to Sweet Water, one of its tributaries, and near to the dividing point, the country becomes more barren all around, being more within that portion of the continent where the sun's influences are not hindered by rains, or even dews, for a great portion of the year. Here, no soil is formd by the decomposition of vegetable or animal matter, for none exists with which to make soil except the wild sage and a few other useless shrubs.

Few animals of any kind dwell here, for want of the means of sustaining life. It may justly be calld a desert country. It should, however, be remarkd that within the distance from Platt to Sweet Water, nearly all the present buffalo range is comprisd, and if the country is a barren waste, how do they receive their support? Along the bottom lands of the Platt and its tributaries, are seen occasional tracts coverd with grass, but these are few compard with the great extent of country over which the buffalo is obligd to ramble for his support. At one season of the year he is seen on Platt and at another on Sweet Water, a distance of more than four hundred miles in extent.

Along the country through which the Sweet Water flows, is seen a range of mountains, calld the Sweet Water range, coverd mostly with a dense forest. On our right are ranges of granite rock of less hight, occasionally divided by intervening valleys. These rocks are naked, having no vegetation upon them except in some of their crevices, where a few vegetables have found a scanty foothold. Within 50 miles of the dividing ridge, these ranges of mountains lower down to an undulating plain, without soil or vegetation, except wild sage, so common on these deserts.

CHAPTER III

The Indians east of the Rocky Mountains, their migratory habits, &c. — The American Fur Company and its shipments — Fort Larimie and location — Saline quality in the earth and the waters of Platt and its tributaries — Independence rock — Daring deed of one of our company.

Twenty-five miles west of St. Josephs, on the emigrant route, is a school for Indians, calld Iowa and Sack Mission Boarding School. It is conducted by a Mr. S. M. Ervin and H. W. Hamilton. During our stay of two or three days at that place, I visited Mr. Ervin at his school-house and dwelling, with a pleasing reception as a stranger, and was shown to the several apartments of the house. It is a building 106 feet in length by about 40 in width, with a basement for cooking and dining-rooms. The other two stories are occupied as school-room, lodging-rooms and dwelling for the superintendent, and in one apartment is a library and printing press. Mr. Ervin pointed me to his scholars, at this time numbering only 26, consisting mostly of girls from ten to twelve years of age, dressd in American costume. These appeard well, and seemd to be a proof that the wild man of the desert is susceptible of cultivation. Unhappily, however, I was informd by a person living there, it is with difficulty youth are persuaded to tarry long enough at the school to acquire any valuable education.

Whilst staying at that place, Mr. Ervin came into our camp and preachd a sermon to the emigrants, and whilst there he publicly declard that we should pass no nation of Indians on our route to Oregon more vicious than those of that place. We however met with no difficulty nor lost any property by them, though one of them had the boldness to say to one of the emigrants —

"Me good to steal horses!"

To which the emigrant replied —

"You must not steal our horses."

The Indian still farther announced —

"Ah, me good to steal horse."

The Indians at this place receive a very good support in consequence of the large amount of land under cultivation by the care and superintendence of the mission.

Those Indians located at Grand Island, calld the Pawnee tribe, are at present a feeble race, liable to be driven about by the Sioux at all times. They are poor, and under the necessity of stealing what buffalo meat and robes they need for their support, and whenever they are discoverd by a band of Sioux rangers, they are obligd to flee for their safety to some other place. Their pressing necessity for food and clothing makes them more inclind to trouble the emigrant trains than they otherwise would, and whenever they meet with a train that is feeble in numbers, they fall on them and plunder their food and clothing.

The day before we arrivd at Grand Island, a band of Sioux rangers discoverd some Pawnees on the banks of the Platt, drying and preparing buffalo meat for their winter's stock of provisions. They enterd their camp and drove them away so suddenly, that in their wild flight they were obligd to throw away robes and other property, which was strewd along the road 15 or 20 miles' distance. By this circumstance we passd the Pawnees without seeing an individual Indian.

The Sioux are probably the strongest nation east of the South Pass. They range from Fort Larimie eastward to the Missouri river. Near Ash Hollow on the Platt, we passd two bands of them not many miles distant from each other, consisting of 40 or 50 lodges in each. Their lodges are made by setting up small poles in a conical form and covering them with buffalo skins. Some of them are quite large, requiring from 10 to 15 buffalo skins to inclose them. In the center of these their fires are built. The smoke issues at the top of this conical-shapd edifice, through which a small opening is left for that purpose. Around these fires whilst in their lodges, the Indians sit or recline upon the ground, without seats of any kind, or any thing at all, except sometimes flag matresses or the pelts of some animals.

When they wish to prepare for the reception of company of a public nature, they form a semi-circle on the ground with their chiefs or heads of bands in the center of the arch of the half-circle, which renders them conspicuous to all. On our approach to the first of these bands, we found them seated in a semi-circular form, with their two chiefs, Whirlwind and Badwoon, in the center of this arch, with the American flag erected within and in front of the chiefs, ready to receive us, having been apprisd of our coming several days beforehand by an Indian trader by the name of Richards, who had traveld with us much of the way from St. Josephs to that place. He having gone ahead, arrivd at the band several days before us, informing them that we were coming and advising them to peace, with the expectation of receiving a gift from us as indicative of friendship. Accordingly they spread robes and blankets on the ground within the half-circle, upon which the emigrants bestowd their gifts of flour, corn meal, beans, bacon, and every such thing, as they pleasd to give. While in the act of doing this, occasional acclamations were heard from the red audience, especially when a larger panful of flour than common was presented.

After our company had ceasd to present their gifts, two or three men started from the circle to make a distribution of the gift, which was bestowd upon the heads of families. This was an amusing sight. Some would present a dish to receive their gift, others the corner of a blanket, and others again would hold out the skirt of an old filthy coat to receive a little flour. Presently all receivd their several gifts, and so we parted in friendship.

The night previous to our arrival at this band, we had encampd about 2 miles distant, though in sight of their lodges. In the morning, after our teams were ready for starting, our captain orderd the train to keep close together, with their guns where they could lay their hands on them at a moment's warning, if necessary, and no one should speak to an Indian except himself till we should pass the reach of danger, as there was no possible way to pass this band excepting through their camp, and as the advice of former emigrants was to guard against the treachery of the Indians. Unfortunately for me, as some would think, I had neither gun, pistol nor bowie-knife with me, but the young man with whom I traveld, having a spare pistol presented it to me, saying—

"Here, take this, and the captain says you must go to his wagon and get a hatchet, so that you may defend yourself and others."

I told him as we had about 2 miles to travel before we should come to them, and as I had no convenient way of carrying it, except in my hand, he had better carry it till we arrivd there, and then I would take it. But this was the last I saw of the pistol at that place. When our teams arrivd at the camp, we all halted, and one man ran one way and another man another way, talking and trading with the Indians, and preparing to give them presents.

These bands migrate with the roaming buffalo, for on him depends their support. At this time they were here, drying buffalo meat for their winter supply, and also preparing robes for sale, though their station is most of the time at Fort Larimie. The flesh of the buffalo is cut into thin pieces and dried in the sun without salt, and this is their principal food. They have no flour except what little they procure of the emigrants while passing to Oregon. In this waste country the plow is not seen to greet the soil, and the poor Indian has nought for his support but what nature alone provides. These Indians are better dressd, and may be considerd more wealthy, if their property can be calld wealth, than Indians west of the Rocky Mountains.

The American Fur Company, which has its posts of trade located at different points east of the Rocky Mountains, are at present in a somewhat prosperous state. I was informd by the Principal at Fort Larimie, that the company shipd from Fort Pier, a point on a tributary of the Missouri river, the year 1847, more than 80,000 buffalo robes, between 11,000 and 12,000 of which were obtain at Fort Larimie, besides a great amount of other peltry. But as the country is gradually drying up and buffalo becoming less abundant, this source of profit will at length fail.

Fort Larimie is located at Larimie fork of Platt river, a mile or two above its confluence with that river. There is nothing interesting about the fort. It is built of sun-dried bricks, with timbers sufficient to support the bricks and form the doors and windows, and done in the coarsest manner. Within this wall, which is about 12 or 14 feet high, are the dwellings and other necessary rooms for the accommodation of the fort. Within this area, also, stands a large rude press, for pressing robes and peltry for market. In another apartment is a yard for horses and cattle. What is most attractive is, within these dwellings are seen the white man and the rusty-looking Indian woman, living lovingly together, whilst the little papooses are playing together as happily. Without these mud walls are seen no appendages. The eye can rest on nothing all around but a dreary waste, an uncultivated country.

On advancing up the Platt and its tributary, Sweet Water river, the traveler's attention is attracted by a kind of salt he occasionally sees upon the ground along the road, which by examining he finds to possess strong alkaline properties. The waters of the Platt and Sweet Water rivers are also impregnated so strongly that whenever the rivers are so low as to disclose the sand-bars long enough for them to dry upon their surfaces, this salt is seen abundantly upon them.

A few miles east of Independence rock, along our route, we saw several ponds, or small lakes, with an incrustation of this salt several inches thick. These places the emigrants call saleratus lakes, from the known fact that it has the property of raising bread.

Advancing a few miles, we come to Independence rock.—This rock is hardly worthy of notice, except for the many inscriptions made upon it by emigrants. It is a coarse granite rock about 100 feet high, covering about 20 acres of ground, standing alone and near enough to our road to read its inscriptions on passing it.

About 4 miles west of Independence rock, the Sweet Water passes through a gap of precipitous rocks 300 feet high, where is a cascade of short distance. This gap is narrow and formd along its sides with several crevices of circular and chimney shape, from top to bottom. In one of these a man of our company, by the name of Brock, descended. Whilst the train was slowly passing along, several men of our company left the train for the purpose of passing through this gap along the sides of the waterfall. On their approach at this place, they stood viewing the scenery around, whilst one of them, looking up, saw a man in the act of descending through one of these frightful openings, at a distance of more than 200 feet above their heads. Mr. Brock had passd around to the top of the rocks alone, to view the scenery, and finding one of these places, attempted a descent. He began the descent without knowing that any human being stood to witness his hazardous undertaking. This opening was so wide in some places that he could with difficulty reach from one side to the other without losing his perpendicular position, and oftentimes he was obligd to hold on to the rocks by his fingers, where they projected not more than an inch. In this alarming situation of Mr. Brock, his comrades below stood looking at him, without daring to speak, with intense anxiety for his safety, till he had accomplishd his entire descent.

CHAPTER IV

Remarks of the writer relative to his Journal en route to Oregon—The Journal.

As I had at one time thought of making a separate history of my every day's travels from St. Josephs to Oregon city, in pamphlet form, in order to benefit those who might desire to have a knowledge of the route and its several distances from place to place, at little cost, I determined to keep as accurate an account of the distances I traveld every day, together with such remarks in a condensed form as might be deemd necessary to guide the traveler to Oregon, as the circumstances of the case would admit. I therefore commencd my reckoning of distances from day to day by the rotation of a wagon-wheel, at St. Josephs, and kept it up unceasingly till I arrivd at Oregon city. But finding this mode of writing somewhat inconvenient, and thinking, likewise, that the history of my travels might not be altogether uninteresting, although at somewhat more cost, I have concluded to insert them in this place with my journal of travels and such incidents as may occur in my absence from home.

On the 25th of April, 1848, I crossd the Missouri river at St Josephs into the Indian territory, with several wagons of emigrants, who intended to travel out a short distance and organize for the route. This day we have traveld as far as the bluffs of the river, a distance of 5 miles, and encampd for the night.—The next day we pursued our journey as far as Musketoe creek, a distance of 8 miles, where we encampd. Next day, Friday, 27th, we organizd into a company of 15 or 20 wagons, with such regulations as we deemd necessary for our safety through the Indian country, and tarried there for the night.

Saturday, April 28, we proceeded on our journey a distance of 12 miles, to the Ioway Mission Boarding-School.

25

The 29th and 30th of April, we tarried at the mission.

Monday, May 1, we traveld 15 miles.

Tuesday, May 2—20 miles.

Wednesday, May 3—15 miles, to Nemahaw creek.

Thursday, May 4, we staid at the same place.

Friday, May 5—13 miles over a very crooked road.

Saturday, May 6—20 miles.

108

Sunday, May 7—14 miles to camp, 4 miles to Blue creek, and 10 more to camp.

Monday, May 8—20 miles to Wyatt, fork of Blue.

Tuesday, 9th—14 miles to Walnut creek, or Sandy.

Wednesday, 10th—18 miles, at Little Fork of L. Sandy.

174

Thursday, 11th—11 miles, at Blue creek.

Friday, 12th—12 miles, yet at Blue.

Saturday, 13th—9 miles, still on Blue creek.

206

Sunday, 14th—10 miles. Here on Blue our company killd a buffalo, for the first.

Monday, 15th—12 miles to camp on a small fork of Blue. Feed has not yet been sufficient to give our cattle a full supply. At this place a few wagons, which had been traveling behind us, came up and joind our party, making in all about thirty wagons.

Tuesday, 16th—28 miles to camp. Twenty brought us to Platt river, and 8 more to camp on banks of Platt river.

256

Wednesday, 17th—22 miles up the south side of Platt.

Thursday, 18th—15 miles to City du Chien, at Plumb creek. Here is the first saline appearance we saw on the ground.

Friday, 19th—Staid at the same place.

293

Saturday, 20th—18 miles to camp on Platt river. Wood and pasturage scarce.

Sunday, 21st—25 miles. Little grass.

Monday, 22d—25 miles along under the bluffs of the river to camp. No wood here, except a few willows, for cooking. It raind all this day, and all the night following.

Tuesday, 23d — The severe storm of the previous night drove our cattle a considerable distance to the bluffs, by which means we did not get them all till three o'clock. We traveld only two miles to-day.

Wednesday, 24th — 12 miles to the crossing of South Fork of Platt. The confluence of the two streams is about 18 miles below the crossing. The intermediate high ridge begins about two miles below the crossing, where probably was once their confluence. This fork at this place is about half a mile wide, and the quicksands gave way so rapidly under our cattle's feet, that we found it necessary to travel quickly over it, for fear of sinking deeply into it. By my reckoning here, the distance from St. Josephs to the crossing is 375 miles. After we crossd the river, we traveld five miles up the north side of the river and encampd for the night without any wood for cooking our food, except a few small willows.

380

Thursday, 25th — 18 miles to camp, one mile and a half west of where the bluffs come to the river.

Friday, 26th — 22 miles to camp, one mile and a half west of where the old road crosses over to the North Fork of Platt. Grass good, the best we have had. No wood.

420

Saturday, 27th — 22 miles to camp on the North Fork of Platt river. Eighteen miles of the route was over a beautifully undulating prairie. Rest of the way, about two miles down into Ash Hollow, to North Platt, rugged, and even dangerous for wagons to pass. Four miles up the river brought us to camp, where we had no wood except what we carried from Ash Hollow.

442

Sunday, 28th — 11 miles up Platt river, over a sandy road, and passd a village of Sioux Indians.

453

Monday, 29th — 17 miles to-day. Sandy road, no wood. Burnt buffalo excrement for cooking.

Tuesday, 30th — 13 miles to camp on Platt. Six miles south of this camp stands Babel towr. It is a precipitous bluff of clay, containing lime enough to give some degree of hardness to it, 600 feet above the bed of the creek that passes near its base on the south side of it. Near to this stands another, nearly equal in hight, but inferior in size.

Wednesday, 31st—21 miles to camp on Platt. 14 to Chimney rock, and 7 more to camp. Chimney rock is of the same material as Babel towr, and is fast crumbling down.

504

June 1st—34 miles to camp on Horse-Shoe creek, 8 miles to where the road leaves the river and passes into Romantic valley, where the bluffs on the sides of the valley resemble distant cities. At the west end of this valley, the bluffs are calld Scot's bluffs, from the circumstance of a man's having died there by that name. At this place is a spring where emigrants may camp, though the grass is not very abundant. At this place we noond, and passd over the bluffs onward, having a good road to Horse creek, where we campd for the night. From Scot's bluffs, Larimie peak is first seen.

538

2d—15 miles through sand-hills a considerable part of the way, near to Platt, where little grass grows, except wild wormwood and prickly pear. Encampd with plenty of wood for fuel.

3d—17 miles, most of the way over a good road, to camp, 1 mile west of Fort Larimie, on Larimie's fork of Platt river.

570

4th, 5th and 6th—Staid at the same place, and shod several oxen, which had become lame by traveling. However, as the road some of the way after that, provd worse than any we had passd, and our oxen not becoming lame by traveling over it, we concluded that their lameness must be attributed in part to the alkali over which they so frequently passd. The fort has a blacksmith shop and some few tools, for the use of which our company paid 7½ dollars for one day and a half.

7th—Left Larimie fork about noon, and passd over the bluffs 2 miles to Platt river. From thence we passd on about 4 miles farther and encampd, with plenty of flood wood, of yellow pine and cedar. During the night, it was so cold as to produce ice in our cooking vessels. About 4 miles farther on, is Black Hills Gap, where the river passes through high, precipitous rocks. At this place, also, the Black hills commence.

June 8th—22 miles through the Black hills. Encampd at a spring of the best water west of St. Josephs, near to Platt. Feed very scarce.

9th—20 miles, over a tolerably good road. The waysides are bordered with wild sage. Occasionally we saw the river Encampd on it at night, with but little grass for our cattle. This night, the weather was not very cold.

10th—17 miles. Left Platt early in the morning, and pursued our way through the Black hills, nearly all the forenoon, in a southerly direction towards Larimie peak. Road to-day quite smooth. The country around is almost destitute of vegetation, except the wild sage. Encampd on Big Timber creek.

635

11th—18 miles through the Black hills. Road tolerably good most of the way. Encampd on Mike's Head creek. Have not seen Platt to-day. Before noon we lost sight of Larimie peak, among the hills.

12th—16 miles to camp on Deer creek, near to Platt. Twelve miles brought us to Platt, and 4 more to our camp. At this place we had a plenty of wood, good water and grass for our stock. About noon, we left the Black hills on the north. South of us they are seen stretching along towards the south-west, gradually receding from us.

669

13th—16 miles. Encampd on Platt with plenty of wood. Feed scarce. The wood through this part of the route is cottonwood, and found only bordering the stream.

14th—Staid at the same place, on account of its being exceedingly windy.

15th—5 miles to Platt crossing.

690

At this place the river is about 40 rods wide, and has considerable current. The Mormons from Salt Lake had arrivd a few days previous, and prepard a raft for crossing.

16th—Crossd the Platt, traveld up the north side of it 2 miles, and encampd.

17th—30 miles. Encampd 3 miles east of the Willow spring. About 3 miles east of camp is a spring or two, the alkaline properties of which are strong enough in dry seasons to kill cattle, if allowd to drink freely. I was informd that the Mormons the last year lost more than 50 cattle at this place, by drinking the water of these springs. Five miles of the morning route was along the Platt, to a place calld Red Butes, from their being tingd with iron ore, as are many others through the Black Hill country. At these butes the Black hills terminate, and the road leaves the Platt and passes over to Sweet Water river.

18th—7 miles over a hilly though smooth road to camp, at a small clear spring, though somewhat saline. No wood, burnt buffalo excrement.

19th — 18 miles, 14 to Sweet Water river, 2 miles to Independence rock, and 2 farther to camp. Grass and water, no wood. To-day over a level but mostly sandy road. The country before us and on our left, at a distance, while traveling along, appeard more serrated, but on advancing, the illusion vanishes, and the hills mostly appear only isolated granite rocks of moderate hight, with large intervening valleys.

747

20th — 14 miles to camp on Sweet Water river. Grass, no wood. After traveling 2 miles in the morning, we came to a kanion, where the river passes through a precipitous ledge of rocks, 300 feet high. The water at this place falls over the ragged rocks, which at some distant time had fallen into the stream from above and formd a cascade. To-day, on our left traverses the Sweet Water range of mountains, whilst on our right are ranges of less hight, divided occasionally by intervening valleys.

21st — Staid at the same place.

761

22d — 12 miles over a sandy road to camp on Sweet Water. Good grass, no wood. Frost and ice during the night.

23d — 14 miles over a sandy road. Grass, no wood. About 3 o'clock, came in full view of the Rocky mountains. Ice formd in our cooking vessels during the night.

787

24th — 17 miles over an uneven, sandy road, to camp, on the Sweet Water river. Here the country is a barren waste, except along the river, where a little grass is found. Back from the river, nothing grows but wild sage. At this place, the water of the river is clear. Previous to this, the waters, like those of Platt, have been turbid.

804

25th — 9 miles over a hilly and gravelly road to camp, where is another kanion of the river.

26th — Left the river this morning, and traveld 17 miles over a very hilly road of coarse, sharp gravel stones, and in some places the rocks protrude so as to strain wagons in crossing them. In viewing the country from some of the highest hills in this place, it appears very broken all around. Passd two or three places that would do for camps for small parties. Encampd on a fork of Sweet Water, just above its junction.

27th — 18 miles. Traveld 4 miles, and crossd the Sweet Water river. Here we left it, to see it no more. About 9 miles farther, brought us to the South pass or dividing ridge.

South of the culminating point, at a little distance, stands a solitary high hill, which some call Table rock. On the right, about 12 or 15 miles, are the Wind River peaks, coverd in some parts with snow. Traveld 5 miles farther and encampd on Pacific springs, calld so from the fact that their waters run westwardly into the Pacific ocean. Some grass, no wood.

28th — 19 miles to Little Sandy creek, a fine stream, of sufficient amount of water to carry 4 run of mill stones. We passd over an entire desert, to-day. There is no possible encampment between Pacific springs and this place, and here is no grass, except what borders the stream, a few rods wide on each side of it.

29th — Six miles to Great Sandy creek, over a barren clay road. Fine stream. Little grass, no wood except a few willows. This stream is a branch of the California Colorado river. This is Greenwood's cut-off, which begins a little east of this river, between the two Sandys. The old road is the one leading to Bridger's fort. It is also the one the Mormons took, when they emigrated to Salt Lake. From Big Sandy creek, the place of our nooning, we traveld about 2 miles, to the top of a high point of ground, where stands Colepit rock, a mound 20 or 30 feet high, and perhaps 100 feet around, composd mostly of clay. On the top of this rock, the country can be viewd to a great distance around.

Advancing 8 miles farther, the country appears a level plain all around as far as the eye can reach, except on the north, where the Wind River range stretches far to the north-west. The rest of the day and the following night, we traveld about 15 miles, to a deep valley, dangerous to go down at night.

It may here be remarkd, that it would be safe to remain at Big Sandy creek till 4 or 4½ o'clock in the afternoon, in order that daylight may appear before arriving at this valley, as it seems necessary to travel part of the distance from Big Sandy to Green river in the night, there being no water nor grass on the way from Big Sandy to Green river, a distance of 44 miles.

30th — 19 miles to Green river. After having passd from Sandy to Green river, over a sage plain, destitute of water and grass for our cattle, with four deep and dangerous valleys to descend into on our way, our hearts were gladdend that we were enabld to slake the thirst of our famishing cattle. Here, also, as much of the way past, were several springs issuing from the banks of the river, containing so much alkali as to render them unpleasant to drink. This crossing of Green river is half way from St. Josephs to Oregon city, being 917 miles.

July 1st—Staid at the crossing.

917

2d—9 miles to camp on Salmon Trout branch, 6 or 8 miles above its union with Green river. We gaind but little towards Oregon, to-day, the road being very circuitous and hilly, part of the way.

3d—16 miles over a very hilly road. 10 miles to nooning, where is a tolerably good camp for a small party, 6 miles farther to camp. No wood, little grass, no water except a small spring.

942

4th—10 miles, over a very hilly and stony road, to Ham's fork of Green river. Some grass, no wood but willows. Here were a few Indian lodges of the Snake tribe.

952

5th—14 miles over a very hilly road, and part of it very dangerous to pass. No wood at camp, and but little grass.

6th—Frost in camp, this morning. To-day, we traveld 18 miles and encampd on Bear river, 4 miles west of Smith fork. The hills around us are quite barren. Bear river has a little grass in some places along its bottoms. It is a considerable stream, though not more than three fourths the water that Green river has at the crossing.

7th—11 miles to camp on Thomas' fork of Bear river, about 5 miles above its confluence, by a circuitous route. No wood but willows.

8th—13½ miles over steep mountains, destitute of soil and vegetation, except weeds, to camp on Bear river, where the bottom furnishes a little grass. South of us at a small distance, in a large bottom, is Bear lake, the outlet of which unites with Bear river, a little below camp. The mountains, viewd from camp, seem to form a triangle. East, comes in Bear river. A little east of south, is a long gap in the mountains, where their waters contribute to Bear lake. A little west of north, the valley stretches far away down Bear river.

9th—Staid at the same place, and attended the burial of a young man of our company. To-day, also, are 14 sick persons in our company.

10th—25 miles to camp on Bear river. Passd several fine rills from the mountains, to-day. A very good road down Bear River bottom. The bottom and mountain lands, to-day, assume a more verdant appearance, though the verdure consists mostly of useless shrubs and weeds, except on the skirts of some of the peaks, where they are clothd with timber sparingly. From this camp, snow is seen on the Bear River mountains.

11th—10 miles to Soda springs, and 1 farther to camp, making 11 miles. Have traveld over volcanic rocks, to-day, the first I have seen on our route. Near to camp and north of it, near the base of the mountain, are three small craters, apparently, of extinct volcanoes. They may, however, be the craters of some of those silent springs.

12th—23½ miles to the head waters of Portneuf, a tributary of Snake river. It runs in a very circuitous manner.

1067½

13th—21 miles, over a mountainous road, to camp. Little grass, no wood but willows.

14th—16 miles to camp, about 4 miles east of Fort Hall in a large plain, coverd over a considerable portion of it with a heavy growth of wild sage. This plain is very extensive, reaching from north to south, probably nearly 100 miles. The Sheep mountain and three butes are seen from the fort, a considerable distance to the north of it, rising abruptly from the plain. To the east, south and south-west, mountains are seen from the fort, serrating the horizon. The rest of the horizon around presents nearly an unbroken expanse. This plain is waterd with several springs and streams of considerable size, some of them rising from the level plain and passing on to join the waters of the Snake or Lewis river. The Snake is a fine river, rising in the Wind River mountains, north of Fort Hall, and passing near to it in a southerly direction, where it is joind by the Portneuf about 9 miles below the fort, with other tributaries along the plain. Thence, bending its course westwardly for more than 100 miles, after which its course is northward till it falls into the Columbia river.

1104½

15th—4 miles to Fort Hall, and 2 miles farther to camp, on Portneuf creek.

1110½

16th—7 miles to Portneuf crossing, about 25 rods above its confluence with Snake river. At this place, and also below, on Snake river, I gatherd a great quantity of red, yellow and blue currants, the stalks of which grew, in some places, from 10 to 14 feet high.

1117½

17th—12½ miles to camp, at some springs near Snake river. After leaving Portneuf crossing, we passd a mile down Snake River bottom, and came to a slough, bad to cross. Passd about half a mile farther, and came to another bad crossing of a small stream. Thence, down the bottom about 2 miles, to a considerable stream, whose banks were steep and its passage difficult. Thence, about half a mile, to where the road ascends the first terrace above the river bottom. The river bottom along this day's route has considerable grass, furnishing camps at almost any place.

1130

18th—18 miles to camp, on Cascade creek. Two miles to American falls, 10 miles to palaisades, 6 to camp. The water of the American falls does not descend perpendicularly, but like a cascade. The whole descent from the upper to the lower expanse is from 40 to 50 feet, reckond by perpendicular measurement. The rocks about the falls appear volcanic, though some of them show marks of stratification. The table lands here close in, so as to make the bottom lands draw to a point at the falls. Below the falls, the table lands border the river, and being entirely destitute of grass, render encampments difficult, much of the way.

19th—8 miles to Cassia creek. No wood. At this camp, the California road leaves the Oregon trail to the right hand. West of camp, and near to it, is a range of basaltic trap rocks, of a prismatic and columnar structure, the fairest specimens of basalt I have seen. Range about 60 feet high above the creek.

20th—16 miles over a district of basaltic rocks, slightly hidden from sight by a thin layer of clay, though in many places they protrude so as to render traveling with wagons irksome. Camp on Marsh or Swamp creek. No wood, plenty of grass bordering the creek. Country around, both mountains and plains, destitute of soil. On the plain, is the famd sage. On the mountains, are clusters of inferior cedar growth. Rest of the mountains totally barren.

21st—11½ miles, over a dry and dusty plain, to camp, on Snake river, about 2 miles above the mouth of Goose creek. Here is a narrow bottom, which furnishes a little coarse grass. No wood. River here about ¼ of a mile wide.

1183½

22d—21 miles. Four miles to Goose creek, 8 miles to the river, a poor place for encamping, 9 miles farther to camp. Grass. No water at this season of the year in this creek. No wood but willows. Forenoon, road was good. Afternoon, rocky.

1204½

23rd—9 miles to Rock creek, so calld from its rocky bottom. Fine little stream. Willows for wood. Good camp.

24th—21 miles to camp. Ten to the crossing of Rock creek. Here the banks are steep and rocky. We noond at this place. Here, also, is grass enough for a small company to camp at. About 4 miles farther on, Rock creek turns to the left, and we saw it no more. At this bend of the creek is a tolerable camp. Seven miles farther brought us to camp, and a miserable one it was, being on the top of Snake River bluffs, a hight of at least 300 feet perpendicular from the river. No grass at this place. Our cattle were driven down a narrow and difficult way, much of it very steep, three-fourths of a mile to the river, where it was bordered in some places by little patches of grass, often not one rod wide. Our cattle were taken up, next morning, with not half a supply during the night.

1234½

25th—16 miles. Eleven miles to Warm Spring creek. Here is but little grass. About 4 miles farther, to Salmon Fall creek. One mile down the creek, to camp, near its mouth. Here is a very good camp. On the north-east side of the river, along here for several miles, are fine springs issuing from the bluffs, some of which would carry the largest flouring mills. They are a curiosity. Supposd to be the waters of the river, spreading out into the country above the American falls, and passing along between the basaltic rock above, and another stratum below, till they arrive at this place, where they are dischargd into the river. The evidence that they are the waters of the river appears to be derivd from the fact, that the river between the falls and this place has not more than half the water in it that it has above the falls.

26th—6 miles. Five miles to first rapids of Salmon falls, 1 more to camp. But little grass at this place, and that is mostly on a small island or two. Salmon falls is more a cascade than fall, except in one place, where it falls a few feet perpendicularly. Also calld Fishing falls. The whole cascade is more than a mile in length. To this place the Indians resort to obtain salmon, which at some seasons of the year are tolerably plenty, having come from the ocean up the Columbia river, to the mouth of Snake river, whence they find their way to this place.

1256½

27th—24½ miles to camp, on Snake river. To obtain this camp, we left the road a mile and a half back, and followd a dry branch down to this place. To-day, we traveld over a dry sage plain, though we had a tolerably good road. At this place, and even farther east, are seen the relics of wagons of former emigrants, strewd along the road. Boxes, bands, tire, and all parts of the irons of wagons, left behind.

1281

28th—2 miles from where we left the road, yesterday, to the old crossing of Snake river. At the crossing, are two small islands, which furnish a little grass, Encampd 2½ miles farther on, where is little grass. No wood for fuel. Along the river at this place, is a kind of grass so salt that cattle will eat it only as they stand in need of salt. The leaves of this grass grow about 3 inches high, and the seed-bearing stalk is from 6 to 10 inches in hight. It grows along the river bottoms, in small patches. I do not know any name for it, and therefore denominate it *salt grass*, as other grasses will grow amongst it, that are perfectly fresh.

29th—12 miles, over as rough and stony a road, along the banks of Snake river, as ever I traveld. One wagon was broken, to-day, and left to be totally destroyd by those that came after us.

1297½

30th—11 miles to camp. Grass not very good. About two miles back, grass might be had by driving the cattle on to an island, in the river. Road sandy during forepart of the route, to-day, and during the afterpart, good.

31st—11½ miles. Six and a half miles to Salt Grass creek, a name given from the abundance of salt grass growing there. A tolerable camp might be had at that place. The creek soon passes among the bluffs, in a northerly direction, and unites with Snake river, about 5 miles below where we are campd. Grass is plenty at this place, but it is almost impossible to obtain any thing of which to make fires.

1320

August 1st—19½ miles, over a very level plain, most of the way, and near to the river, to camp, on Grease Wood creek, about a mile above its mouth. No good camp can be had along this day's route, till our present one, which is not very good. Between camp and Snake river, the little stream on which our camp is located passes through two crags of basaltic rock, much crumbled down by time. Rock, east of creek, shows marks of excessive volcanic violence. Volcanic cinders, rocks half melted, chimneys where smoke has issued, and in fact, every mark of Vulcan's blacksmith shop is here displayd.

2d—24 miles to camp on Snake river, at the mouth of a small dry branch. Grass scarce. No place for encamping, short of this place, except at 8 miles from last night's camp, where a small stream affords very little grass. Our way, to-day, has been over a very uneven and dusty road. We ascended one hill, so steep and sandy, that we were obligd to double our teams to surmount it.

1363½

3d—4 miles to camp, on Snake river, and drove our cattle on to a small island.

4th—9 miles to camp, on Snake river, 7½ miles to Hot springs, 1½ to camp. The water of these Hot springs, at their source, is scalding hot. We crossd them both, a short distance from their source, and as they are not very far apart, it is probable that their fountain is together. They are much mineralized.

5th—14½ miles, through a sultry hot day, over a desert plain and dusty road, to camp, on Snake river. No good camp could be had short of this place, to-day. During the day, we could discover a visible lowering down of the mountains on each side, towards the confluence of Boyce and Owyhe rivers and the Snake, where their valleys unite and form an extensive plain. Salt grass still continues along the river bottom. We, to-day, lose sight of the basaltic rocks, so long witnessd on our right hand and on our left. They reach from the American falls nearly to this place, and as they appear to be thinner on advancing westward, it is thought by some that the lava of which they are formd, flowd in that direction. It is said that the Indians of this place are snakes in the grass, but it is much to be regretted that the river is not a snake in the grass, whilst our cattle are in so starving a condition.

6th—19 miles to camp on Owyhe river, about 4 miles above Fort Boyce. Not very good grass at this place.

1410

7th—Traveld one mile and a half down Owyhe river, and encampd.

8th—16 miles, over a good road, to camp, on Malheur (pron. malare) river. Grass plenty. No firewood but willows. At this place, Mr. Meek attempted a cut-off to Oregon city, by following up the course of this river south, for some distance, and then directing his course westward, till he should arrive at Willamet valley, south a considerable distance from Oregon city. His attempt proved a failure, with the loss of considerable property and the lives of some of his company. It is said that there were nearly 200 wagons in his train.

Our route to-day, from last night's camp to Malheur river, leaves Fort Boyce 3 miles to the right. The fort is located in a pleasant place, on the bank of Snake river, just below the union of the Owyhe and Boyce with the Snake. The river at this place is near a quarter of a mile wide, and the only means of ferrying it is a canoe brought from the river Payette, 250 miles from this place.

1427½

9th—25 miles to camp, on Birch creek. 13 miles to a sulphur spring, where we noond. This distance is up an arm of the Malheur, though dry at the time. Its course is through a level flat, from one to two miles wide, having high ranges of land on each side. From Sulphur spring, the road ascends rapidly to its highest point, a mile or two farther on, where the country can be viewd for a considerable distance all around. Reflecting upon such a wonderful scenery as is here on every side displayd, the mind can hardly appreciate the amount of dynamics adequate to displace and disrupt the surface of the earth so immensely. It appears like a great harrow, fit only for Hercules to use in leveling off the surface of some planet.

10th—8 miles to Burnt river, (probably from the naked and reddend appearance of the mountains through which it passes.) Three miles of the morning route brought us once more to Snake river, where we saw it for the last time. Remaining 5 miles over a somewhat hilly road to camp, on Burnt river, but a small stream at this place. On viewing the river and its small flats bordering it, from camp, it appears wholly environd by rugged, jagged mountains, in close contiguity. Oh, when shall I view, once more, a verdant landscape! One thousand miles of naked rocks! Landscape without soil! River bottoms with scarcely grass enough to support emigrant teams. Who can but think of his native land and the "old oaken bucket"?

1460½

11th—13 miles to camp on Burnt river. No good camp short of this, and this not very good. For 5 or 6 miles of our morning route up the river, the road was very rough and stony, and it crosses the creek seven times within that distance. Remainder of the day's travel was more easily performd, though more hilly, yet smooth. South of camp and near to it, ascends a mountain, the height of which, as nearly as I could measure, with the limited means I had, is about 1300 feet above the bed of Burnt creek. Along this stream emigrants have formerly been much intimidated through fear of sudden attacks from Indians. It is very densely shrouded much of the way with balm of Gilead, alder, hawthorn, and various kinds of shrubbery, so that the Indians could secrete themselves, till the near approach of an emigrant train, and then with a sudden rush from the thicket, frighten the teams and kill many of the emigrants. However, we saw no Indians along this river.

12th—4 miles over a worse road than yesterday afternoon, and crossd the creek five times.

1477½

13th—16 miles to camp on a tributary of Burnt river. Soon after having started in the morning, we crossd the principal stream of Burnt river, for the last time. A little farther on, we came to a small right hand tributary coming from the north, which we followd up about 2 miles, crossing it 8 times. We then left it, winding our way over the mountains westwardly, crossing two or three other small tributaries, till we arrivd again upon the Burnt river bottoms, not more than 8 miles in a straight line from last night's camp. At this place we noond, after having passd over a hilly, though smooth road. Here emigrants might tarry for the night. One mile further on we crossd North fork, and upset one wagon at the crossing. Our course was now nearly west, up a mountain, till we arrivd at a branch of the North fork. Passing on a mile or more, we encampd for the night. Grasses along the bottom here are coarse, consisting of wild wheat, rye, and wild chess. Mountain grasses here are the bunch grass, as it is calld, but at this time so dry and dead that cattle do not love it. The hills at the sources of the Burnt river, among which they ramify in all directions, like the blood vessels in the human system, are composd measurably of a slaty rock, which decomposes into loose material more readily than the hard basaltic rocks of Snake river. Occasionally, however, graphic granite is here seen to protrude above the hills.

14th—20 miles to camp, at Lone Pine stump, now nearly obliterated by fires set to it by emigrants, in the valley of Powder river. Here is the bed of a small stream, where there is water at some seasons of the year, though dry now, except in stagnant ponds. Grass is tolerably plenty along this little branch. No wood at this place to be obtaind for cooking. Road, to-day, hilly but smooth. At about 6 miles, emigrants might camp. Here, we left the waters of Burnt river, and passd over the hills to Powder river. Powder River valley, east of camp, still retains the old character of desert and sage plain.

1513½

15th — 14½ miles to camp, on west branch in west valley of Powder river. Nine miles to Powder river, down by a circuitous route, along the river, 2 miles to first crossing. Thence across the plain to second fork or crossing, 2½ miles. One mile farther to west fork or third crossing. In all, 14½ miles to camp. East valley of Powder river is a spacious plain, very level, and would be as handsome a valley as my feet ever trode upon, were it coverd with the rich grasses of the eastern states. At each of the three crossings here mentiond, which unite a short distance below us and form the principal Powder river, is seen in small patches, a luxuriant growth of the well known grass, red top. As we advance, the climate changes. In camp, this morning, was seen ice in our cooking vessels, and by 10 we were uncomfortably warm. On our left, the Powder River mountains, close by which the river finds it way, are clothd with timber, nearly down their declivities to their base. On our right they yet are naked, Indians around us are burning, as fast as verdure becomes dry enough, which at this time, renders the air so smoky, that we can see but a short distance.

16th — 15 miles to camp, at the head of Grand Round valley. After traveling a short distance, this morning, from the last crossing of Powder river, we ascended a short rise. We then proceeded over a smooth road of moderate descent, till we came to a small branch of Powder river, at the foot of a hill, where several small rivulets are seen to issue from the hills round about. This is about 8 miles from the last crossing. Here is a tolerable encampment. The rest of the way to Grand Round hollow, a distance of 7 miles further, is over a hilly and some part of the way, very stony road. At 10½ miles from the crossing, emigrants might also encamp for the night, there being a little water and some grass along a small run. Grand Round valley is extensive. It is surrounded with high hills, coverd with bunch grass, except occasional patches of yellow pine. Along our road, this valley is rich, coverd with various kinds of grasses, though entirely dead much of the way across the upper end of the valley at this time, no rains having fallen here lately.

17th — 15 miles to camp, on Grand Round river. Eight miles across the head of the beautiful Grand Round valley, to a small branch, where emigrants might camp for the night, at the foot of the Blue mountains bordering the valley. From thence, we wound our way over the steep and rugged mountains, racking and straining our wagons, the distance of 7 miles farther, to the deep and lonely dell, where the Grand Round river is struggling and forcing its way through its narrow passage, down to the beautiful valley, Grand Round. Over this day's route, the mountains have as rich a soil as the valley, till near the dell, where the red mountain soil is seen. Where we are campd, the dell is narrow, and furnishes but little grass. It is remarkable for loudness of sound, when a gun is fired. Rocks of these mountains, volcanic.

1558½

18th—10½ miles, over a very uneven district of volcanic rocks and mountain soil, to camp, on one of the highest peaks of the Blue mountains on our route. Country, to-day, becomes more densely timberd all around and along our road, overshadowing it in many places with yellow pine, fir and spruce hemlock. Have passd several deep cuts, to-day, so steep that teams were necessarily doubld to ascend out of them, and some of them were dangerous and difficult. Our camp is located on the side of a high ridge, in a small opening, nearly one fourth of a mile above its base, where we were obligd to descend, to obtain water for cooking. From this high ridge, it is said, Mt. Hood can be seen, but at this time it is so smoky, that we can see but a little distance.

1569

19th—10 miles, over the western declivity of the Blue mountains, moderate in descent, and tolerably smooth most of the way to camp, in a small opening, a little larger than our carelle, calld Lee's encampment. Here, two men met us, from Fort Waters, where the late murders were committed, with news that we had nothing to fear from hostile Indians, any farther on our route. This gave great encouragement to the timorous emigrants. Accordingly,

20th—We descended the western declivity of the Blue mountains, part of the way over volcanic scoria, to camp, on Umatilla river. About 12 miles of the first part of this day's route, was through a timberd district of pine, hemlock and fir, loaded, many of them, with pendant moss. On leaving the timber, we ascended a hill, a mile or more, to Mount Prospect, the last high point before descending the bluffs to the river. I name the hill, from its commanding a view of the whole western horizon, to a great distance around.

On Prospect hill is a cluster of rocks, which, with a little help of the imagination, can be easily construed into Vulcan's blacksmith shop, where all the cinders so profusely spread over the Blue mountains, were made. On retiring, he left his forge loaded with the cinders of his last blast, as a memorial of his great ambition.

Three and a half miles more, down the bluffs, brought us to camp, making in all, this day, 16½ miles.

1595½

21st—Down Umatilla river, near to crossing, 10 miles. Country here entirely prairie, and very undulating.

22d—Crossd the river, half a mile below camp, and passd about two miles on the flat. Ascended the bluff, and passd over the prairie about 14 miles, to the river, down the river two miles to camp, making in all 18½ miles. Prairie, to-day, uneven, and of poor soil.

1624

23d—14½ miles to camp, on Alder creek. Five miles to second crossing of Umatilla, 8½ miles to Alder creek, up the same one mile to camp. Little grass, no wood but fine willows. In this day's travel, two miles might have been savd, by crossing the river at camp, but to avoid sandy traveling, emigrants go down the river some farther. This is Whitman's cut-off.

24th—18½ miles, over a poor tract of the Columbia River valley, to camp, at the foot of a hill, by a spring, calld Well spring, rising in the center of a large mound of decayd vegetation, and sinking suddenly again, within a few feet of where it issues. Noond, to-day, on the battle-ground of the 24th February, 1848, between Oregon soldiers and the Cayuse Indians. No grass nor water exists along this day's route, where emigrants might refresh themselves and their weary teams. Fire wood is obtaind two miles east, in a hollow, where are a few scattering cedars. The spring at camp should be watchd during the night, by a strong guard, to keep thirsty cattle from falling into it, out of which they cannot extricate themselves.

25th—13 miles, over a miserably poor and uneven country, to Quesnell's creek. Down the creek one mile, in order to obtain water, where camp is located.

1670

26th—Staid at camp. Morning cold. Found there was ice in our cooking vessels, though weather became warm during the day.

27th—Returnd up the creek to the crossing, though on the west side of the flat. From the east side of the flat, to-day's reckoning commences, and crosses over to Beaver fork of John Day's river, a distance of 20½ miles. No camp can be had between the two places, though a small spring exists, two miles east of camp. Most of the way to-day, the road has been good, through a long, level valley.

28th—7 miles to crossing of John Day's river. Way down Beaver fork, very rocky, and road crosses it 4 times.

1697½

29th—Down John Day's river, half a mile. Then ascended the bluff, about one mile, up a narrow, winding, rocky ravine, the worst we had ever traveld. On the top of this bluff, the road divides, one leading to the Columbia river. The other, at the left, is the one we took. From the top of this bluff, the road, the remainder of the day, was smooth to camp, at a lone spring among the bluffs. Distance to-day, about fifteen miles. Grass enough for a small band. No wood. About two miles east, up a ravine a short distance to the left, there are two small springs, where a small party might camp for the night. No wood.

1712½

30th—25 miles to camp, on the western declivity of the dividing ridge, between John Day's and Deshutes river, at the upper end of a ravine, where was a little grass, but no wood, and no water for cattle. We staid through the night, without supper, and left next morning, without breakfast.

31st—Traveld about 5 miles, to the crossing of Deshutes or Fall river. Here, we breakfasted in a deep chasm, almost as difficult of descent and ascent, as the valley of Sindbad the sailor, with nearly precipitous rocks, from 1000 to 1500 feet high, on every side. Afternoon employd in calking wagon-boxes, to ferry our goods across the river.

Friday, Sept. 1st—All day employd in getting our goods across the river, with the help of several Indians. River at the crossing, about seven rods wide, with considerable current.

2d—Whilst watching some of our wagons on the bank of the river, till others could be taken up the bluffs, I was led to the following reflections upon the miserable condition of the poor, degraded-looking Indians at this place—

THE INDIANS OF DESHUTES

"That Indian, whose untutord mind
Sees God in the clouds, or hears him in the wind—
Whose soul, proud science never taught to stray"
Far as the glittring sun, or other orbs of day,
Lives far retird—a kanion deep, a solitary dell,
A gloomy shade—'tis there he deigns to dwell.
What is his food, when naught but rocks around
Are seen? No fields of plenty there do clothe the ground.
His raiment, also scant, to shield his naked form,
No robes of beasts, nor pelts, nor furs, to guard him from
the storm.

And when with food he chance to break his fast,

He finds no wood to cook his limited repast.

Alas, what then? The salmon and the salmon trout,

In that mad stream, are seen to gambol all about.

By him prepard upon the rocks, or hung on slender poles,

Not far above, on steep decline, where furious water rolls,

He dries his food, and thus 'tis savd from future harm.

'Tis nearly all he has of food—his clothes, they still are less,
with which to keep him warm.

Now, why should man, poor wretched man, receive such
prompt reply,

That when he broke the law of God, 'twas sure that he must
die?

Yet linger first awhile, still wretched and forlorn,

To glean an almost naked earth, 'mongst thistle and the
thorn?

'Twas done to show that God is just, and true to all intent,—

That man a lesson here might learn, and thus to him repent.

Nine miles from Deshutes, over the rocky bluffs, brought us to another resting-place, on an arm of Deshutes, flowing from the mountains, in the direction of Mount Hood. Five miles from Deshutes, was a spring, where emigrants sometimes camp, but at this time the Indian ponies had eaten off all the grass. We therefore passd on to our present camp.

1751½

3d—12½ miles to camp, on a small tributary of Deshutes, at Barlow's gate—all but the gate, though he was found sitting there at the receipt of custom, allowing each emigrant wagon to pass his road through the Cascade mountains, at the moderately healthy sum of five dollars each, which the Government of Oregon had authorized him to receive. But, as miserable a road as it was, thanks be to Mr. Barlow for his energetic movement in opening a way through so rough a district as the Cascade mountains.

Several small streams were passd to-day, though no camps could well be made on them, for want of grass, except the first, which had a very little.

1764

4th—Staid at the same place.

5th—Over the rocky hills, 12 miles to camp, on a muddy arm of Deshutes, flowing from Mount Hood. Ten and a half miles to the arm, 1½ up the same to camp. No grass for our stock.

6th—3 miles up Deshutes valley, to Palmer's cabin. In consequence of having lost some of our cattle in the thick and almost impenetrable forest, our day's drive was short. A little below Palmer's cabin, are signs of very rich bog iron ore. I afterwards found other places of iron ore along the road, by which I was satisfied that the Cascades abound in iron.

1779

7th—10 miles, over the dividing ridge, to camp, at a small flat prairie on our left, from which Mount Hood is seen, a few miles distant, towring high above its neighbor mountains.

1789

8th—10 miles to camp. No grass. Chaind our oxen to trees, and cut a few birch limbs for them. Passd, to-day, what is calld Laurel hill. It is steep and dangerous.

9th—6 miles, down Muddy fork of Sandy, to camp. Drove our cattle across the stream, and found some grass for them. This has been a rainy day.

10th—15 miles, most of the way over a good road, especially on the ridge, calld by some, "Devil's Back-Bone."

11th—8 miles, over a hilly road, down to the first settlement, at the west foot of the Cascade mountains. One mile to the last crossing of Sandy creek, 7 more to camp.

1828

12th—12 miles to camp.

13th—6 miles to Oregon city.

1846

ADVICE TO EMIGRANTS

CHAPTER V

Necessary outfits for emigrants to Oregon or California,
taken from Palmer's Journal of Travels to Oregon—
Additional advice by the Author.

For burthen wagons, light four-horse or heavy two-horse wagons are the size commonly usd. They should be made of the best material, well seasond, and should in all cases have falling tongues. The tire should not be less than one and three fourths inches wide, but may be advantageously usd three inches; two inches, however, is the most common width. In fastening on the tire, bolts should be usd instead of nails; it should be at least five eighths or three fourths of an inch thick. Hub boxes for the hubs should be about four inches. The skeins should be well steeld. The Mormon-fashiond wagon-bed is the best. They are usually made straight, with side-boards about 16 inches wide, and a projection outward of four inches on each side, and then another side-board of 10 or 12 inches. In this last, set the bows for covers, which should always be double. Boxes for carrying effects should be so constructed as to correspond in hight with the offset in the wagon-bed, as this gives a smooth surface to sleep upon.

Ox teams are more extensively usd than any others. Oxen stand the trip much better, and are not so liable to be stolen by the Indians, and are much less trouble. Cattle are generally allowd to go at large, when not hitchd to the wagons, whilst horses and mules must always be stakd up at night. Oxen can procure food in many places where horses cannot, and in much less time. Cattle that have been raisd in Illinois or Missouri, stand the trip better than those raisd in Indiana or Ohio, as they have been accustomd to eating the prairie grass, upon which they must wholly rely while on the road. Great care should be taken in selecting cattle—they should be from four to six years old, tight and heavy made.

For those who fit out but one wagon, it is not safe to start with less than four yoke of oxen, as they are liable to get lame, have sore necks, or to stray away. One team thus fitted up may start from Missouri with twenty-five hundred pounds, and as each day's rations make the load that much lighter, before they reach any rough road, their loading is much reducd.— Persons should recollect that every thing in the outfit should be as light as the requird strength will permit. No useless trumpery should be taken. The loading should consist of provisions and apparel, a necessary supply of cooking fixtures, a few tools, &c. No great speculation can be made in buying cattle and driving them through to sell, but as the prices of oxen and cows are much higher in Oregon than in the States, nothing is lost in having a good supply of them, which will enable the emigrant to wagon through many articles that are difficult to be obtain in Oregon. Each family should have a few cows, as the milk can be usd the entire route, and they are often convenient to put to the wagon to relieve oxen. They should be so selected that portions of them would come in fresh upon the road. Sheep can also be advantageously driven. American horses and mares always command high prices, and with careful usage can be taken through,—but if usd to wagons or carriages, their loading should be light. Each family should be provided with a sheet-iron stove, with boiler. A platform can easily be constructed at the hind end of the wagon, and as it is frequently quite windy, and there is often a scarcity of wood, the stove is very convenient. Each family should also be provided with a tent, and to it should be attachd good strong cords, to fasten it down.

The cooking fixtures generally usd are of sheet iron—a Dutch oven and skillet of cast metal are very essential. Plates, cups, &c., should be of tinware, as queensware is much heavier and liable to break, and consumes much time in packing up. A reflector is sometimes very useful. Families should each have two churns, one for carrying sweet and one for sour milk.—They should also have one eight or ten-gallon keg for carrying water, one axe, one shovel, two or three augers, one hand-saw, and if a farmer, he should be provided with one cross-cut saw and a few plow-molds, as it is difficult getting such articles. When I left the country, plows cost from twenty-five to forty dollars each. A good supply of ropes for tying up horses and catching cattle, should also be taken.

Every person should be well supplied with boots and shoes, and in fact with every kind of clothing. It is also well to be supplied with at least one feather bed, and a good assortment of bedding. There are no tame geese in the country, but an abundance of wild ones, yet it is difficult procuring a sufficient quantity of feathers for a bed. The Muscovy is the only tame duck in the country.

Each male person should have at least one rifle gun, and a shot gun is also very useful for wild fowl and small game, of which there is an abundance.

The best sized calibre for the mountains is from thirty-two to fifty-six to the pound—but one of from sixty to eighty, or even less, is best when in the lower settlements. Buffaloes seldom range beyond the South Pass, and never west of Green river. The larger game are elk, deer, antelope, mountain sheep or bighorn, and bear. The small game are hare, rabbit, grouse, sage hen, pheasant, quail, &c. A good supply of ammunition is essential.

In laying in a supply of provisions for the journey, persons will doubtless be governd in some degree by their means, but there are a few essentials that all will require.

For each adult, there should be two hundred pounds of flour, thirty pounds of pilot bread, seventy-five pounds of bacon, ten pounds of rice, five pounds of coffee, two pounds of tea, twenty-five pounds of sugar, half a bushel of dried beans, one bushel of dried fruit, two pounds of saleratus, ten pounds of salt, half a bushel of corn meal—and it is well to have a half bushel of corn, parchd and ground—a small keg of vinegar should also be taken. To the above may be added as many good things as the means of the person will enable him to carry, for whatever is good at home is none the less so on the road. The above will be ample for the journey, but should an additional quantity be taken, it can be readily disposd of in the mountains and at good prices, not for cash, but for robes, dressd skins, buckskin pants, moccasins, &c. It is also well for families to be provided with medicines. It is seldom, however, that emigrants are sick—but sometimes eating too freely of fresh buffalo meat causes diarrhœa, and unless it be checkd soon prostrates the individual, and leaves him a fit subject for disease.

The time usually occupied in making the trip from Missouri to Oregon city is about five months, but with the aid of a person who has traveld the route with an emigrating company, the trip can be performd in about four months.

Much injury is done to teams in racing them, endeavoring to pass each other.

Emigrants should make an every-day business of traveling—resting upon the same ground two nights is not good policy, as the teams are likely to ramble too far.

Getting into large companies should be avoided, as they are necessarily compeld to move more tardily. From ten to twenty-five wagons is a sufficient number to travel with safety. The advance and rear companies should not be less than twenty, but between, it may be safe to go with six.

The Indians are very annoying on account of their thieving propensities, but if well watchd, they would seldom put them in practice.

Persons should always avoid rambling far from camp unarmd or in too small parties; Indians will sometimes seek such opportunities to rob a man of what little effects he has about him, and if he attempts to get away from them with his property, they will sometimes shoot him.

There are several points along the Missouri where emigrants have been in the practice of fitting out. Of these, Independence, St. Josephs and Council Bluffs, are the most noted. For those emigrating from Ohio, Indiana, Illinois and northern Missouri, Iowa and Michigan, I think St. Josephs the best point, as by taking that route the crossing of several streams (which at the early season we travel are sometimes very high) is avoided. Outfits may be had at this point as readily as at any other along the river. Work cattle can be bought in its vicinity for from twenty-five to thirty dollars per yoke, cows, horses, &c., equally cheap.

Emigrants should endeavor to arrive at St. Josephs early in April, so as to be in readiness to take up the line of march by the middle of April. Companies, however, have often started as late as the tenth of May; but in such cases they seldom arrive in Oregon until after the rainy season commences in the Cascade range of mountains.

Those residing in northern Ohio, Indiana, Illinois, Michigan, &c., who contemplate traveling by land to the place of rendezvous, should start in time to give their teams at least ten days' rest. Ox teams, after traveling four or five hundred miles in the States, at that season of the year, would be unfit to perform a journey across the mountains; but doubtless they might be exchangd for others, at or near the rendezvous.

Farmers would do well to take along a good supply of horse gears. Mechanics should take such tools as are easily carried; as there are but few in the country, and those are held at exorbitant prices. Every family should lay in a good supply of school books for their children.

Since the advice of Mr. Palmer was given to Oregon emigrants, relating to outfits for the overland route to that country, some advantages have been experiencd by the use of mule instead of ox teams. In the first place, that animal is much more sure-footed than the ox or the horse, and in the next place, he can live on kinds of food that the ox or the horse will not eat, and he will also live on a much less amount. The mule is more hardy than the horse or the ox, and will endure fatigue when the others will faint. Another circumstance which I do not recollect to have seen mentiond by any writer, and which it may not be improper to add in this place, is the failure of oxen upon the emigrant route, from lameness by traveling over ground bestrewn with salts of various kinds, but mostly alkali. To neutralize the alkali so as to prevent the oxen from becoming lame, their hoofs should be rubd with lard or tallow at least twice each day, till the tract of country containing such salt is passd over. It is, however, probable that in a few years the place of oxen will be supplied by the use of mules, though attention will doubtless need to be paid to the hoofs of mules, to keep them sound, as well as of oxen.

If persons wish to leave the States for California by the overland route, earlier than the time mentioned by Mr. Palmer, it would be necessary to leave the States with as much provision for their teams as they could at first well haul, after having first supplied themselves with their own necessary food to last them through their journey. In such case a considerable distance may be overcome before the early production of grasses upon the plains.

A few words by way of advice to persons wishing to go to California to dig for gold, may not be uninteresting here. I have noticed that miners from the States carry to California a great amount of baggage and implements for mining operations at great costs of transportation and removal from one place to another, which I deem wholly unnecessary. This oftentimes enormous expense can be savd from the fact that clothing and mining implements of all necessary kinds are very abundant in California, although at a higher price than in the States, yet still the cost of most articles in the mines will not equal the cost in the States, added to transportation costs from the States to the seat of mining operations in California. I would therefore say that one suit of substantial coarse clothes, and money enough to defray expenses there, is all that is best to carry. The amount of money necessary to defray expenses, by way of the isthmus, from the States to the seat of mining operations in California, cannot at present be less than 200 dollars to each person, at the cheapest mode of traveling. Conveyance by steamer, with best accommodations, will cost not much short of 500 dollars, but in no case, considering contingencies, will it be safe to start with less than 300 dollars.

Another circumstance which I have seen much chanted in the public papers, although not particularly connected with the foregoing information, is the scheme of making a railroad from the States overland to California. I can only speak for one person, and this much it is, that if Whitney knew that out of 2000 miles overland, more than 1500 of it is a waste, barren tract, and likewise much of it very rugged, he might be prepard to think as I do, that the income of such a road would never keep it in repair.

DESCRIPTION OF OREGON

CHAPTER VI

South Pass—Wind River Mountains—Oregon, its three grand divisions.

Having accomplishd my journal of distances from St. Josephs to Oregon city, I begin my history of Oregon with the South Pass and Wind River mountains. From descriptions formerly given by some writers of the South Pass, the reader may be led to suppose that the traveler is to pass through a tremendous gap of the Rocky mountains, walld in with huge rocks on its sides, passable only by traversing the bottoms of a stream of water, which finds its way through the mountains of that place. But instead of such an appearance as that, on arriving at the culminating point, he sees before him, on his left and behind, only an undulating country, difficult probably in many places to pass with wagons, on account of the roughness and unevenness of the surface of the land, but destitute entirely of those cragged cliffs and high towring mountains, which the imagination sometimes pictures out, previous to a perfect vision of a country scenery.

The surface of the land along the emigrant route at the pass, is sufficiently uneven to determine within one rod of the culminating point, after which within a short distance, the road commences a somewhat rapid descent westward three or four miles, to a spring issuing from the hills, calld Pacific spring, because its waters are dischargd westward into the Pacific ocean.

On the right, at the dividing ridge, twelve or fifteen miles north of the emigrant road, terminate the Wind River range of mountains, calld also the Rocky mountains. From their southern extremity to a considerable distance either east or west of the dividing ridge, they are seen to stretch far away to the north-west, towring high and giving rise to several important rivers, which traverse the continent, and terminate, some of them in the Atlantic ocean eastward, and some of them in the Pacific ocean westward. Although these mountains have many lofty peaks, yet I believe none of them are sufficiently high to maintain their glaciers during the whole year, at all times. It is nevertheless true, that some of their chasms and deep ravines upon their north-eastern declivities oftentimes have snow lying in them through the year, yet no point on any one of them, as has been remarkd, is high enough for the existence of a zone of perpetual frost. This position is well corroborated, also, from the fact that forests are seen growing, not only high up their declivities, but entirely upon their summits.

The present country of Oregon, belonging to the U. States, extends from the dividing ridge or natural division of the waters of the continent, to the Pacific ocean westward, and in extent north and south, from lat. 42 deg. north to 49 deg. north. It seems to be divided into three grand divisions, by ranges of parallel mountains from north to south. The dividing summit of the continent on the east, west of the eastern division, are the Blue mountains, separating it from the middle,—and between the middle and western divisions, is the Cascade range of mountains.

CHAPTER VII

The Divisions are separately considerd—The Climate—
Rivers and Agricultural Resources—Mineral and Geological
Character.

The first or eastern division of Oregon can at present be considerd worth
little else than to hold the world together. It, however, furnishes a tolerably
good conveyance towards the ocean for some of the waters of Oregon, that
take their rise in the Rocky mountains and elsewhere along the western
declivity of the continent near to the dividing ridge.

The surface of this division is undulating. Some of its rivers traverse the
country along their beds, from five hundred to more than one thousand feet
below the common surface. Although along the emigrant route this division
measures about seven hundred miles in width, yet its true width may not
much exceed six hundred,—and little else is seen but a country destitute of
soil and vegetation, excepting wild sage, and except also along the rivers
and some of the valleys, where detachd portions of grass are seen. The
valley along the emigrant route, through which the Powder river waters
pass, is a level plain, and it would be a delightsome Eden, had it soil, and
were it coverd with luxuriant grasses.

I am here led to remark, that the analysis of the soil here, made by Col.
Fremont on his way through this valley, to foreign readers might produce
much misunderstanding relative to the soil of the country generally.
Although the analysis here producd may be such as indicates good soil,
yet with a little exaggeration it may be said that another shovelful of earth
would have taken nearly all the soil of the whole valley.

Across the middle division of Oregon by way of the emigrant route,
from Grand Round valley to Barlow's gate, at the east side of the Cascade
range of mountains, is about 212 miles, though probably in a direct course
it would be some less than 200. The Blue mountains traversing this division,
give rise to some rivers that checker its visage, but they are of minor
importance, and nearly dried up in the summer, from the long absence
of rains in those parts. This division compares very well with the eastern,
in point of barrenness and disadvantages generally for the promotion of
settlement and improvements of any kind.

I come now to consider the western division of Oregon—the only one on which settlements of any considerable extent have been effected, although Dr. Whitman succeeded in maintaining a small position on the Walla Walla river, till the fall of 1847, at which time himself and wife were killd by the Indians of his own fostering, growing out of a dissatisfaction relative to his treatment with them. And although it is thought by many that the doctor acted in all good conscience towards them, yet through blind zeal and probably a sectarian influence from other denominations of religionists, they were led to believe that the doctor was taking measures to undermine their liberties, and ultimately to overthrow and destroy them.

From the east side of the Cascade range of mountains westwardly to the Pacific ocean the western division ranges from 150 to 200 miles in width, and extending from north to south through the whole length of the Oregon territory.

In remarking upon the several distinct subjects that come to hand relative to Oregon, I am first led to notice its climate.—The climate of Oregon may be considerd a healthy one, though it is subject to considerable changes from year to year. The summer seasons are generally dry, with warm days and cool nights, from the first of July to the first of October, though the rainy season, as it is calld, does not commence much before November, at which time, and for three or four months after, the land becomes so saturated with water, and the streams so swollen, that little passing is done by the citizens from one place to another.

Soon after the rainy season commences in the valleys, the mountainous portions begin to be coverd with snow, and it continues to accumulate upon them at every successive storm, till in many places the snow becomes nearly thirty feet deep, which lasts until quite the latter part of the succeeding summer, before it entirely disappears.

The winter seasons are very variable. During some of the winters, the grasses of the valleys remain green, garden vegetables are verdant, and but little frost is seen. Others again, for three months, the earth is bound up with frost, and the rivers are frozen over of sufficient thickness to bear passages of considerable burden.

So far as the health of this country is concernd, it is true that some sickness prevails, but it may be in a great measure owing to the physical change in the physiology of the human system, in passing from the States to a country so different in climate. After emigrants become acclimated here, the blood becomes of a bright scarlet red, being much more aerated or oxygenized than exists in the system in any of the southern States of America, and consequently better health may be inferd. At some seasons of the year, along some of the rivers, ague and fever exists, but it is generally of a very mild character, and medicine takes a speedy and salutary effect upon the human system.

The description of the climate here given of Oregon, being applicable to the western division does not in all respects apply to the two eastern divisions. The whole of Oregon lying east, of the Cascade range of mountains, is much drier, having less rains at any time, than the portion lying west of them.

It is often quite cold in winter, and being very dry in summer, renders it truly a desert country.

The rivers of Oregon of any considerable notice, are well known to most readers. Although Columbia river is much the largest in the territory, and produces the greatest drainage of any one, yet it does not by a considerable amount drain all of the waters of Oregon that find their way to the Pacific ocean. Green river, commencing at Fremont's peak, in the Wind river mountains, is the principal source of the great Rio Colerado of Calafornia. The great Sacramento of upper Calafornia, has its principal source in Oregon. Other rivers though less in size, yet nevertheless, rivers that are likely to become rivers of considerable, importance, indent the western coast, and furnish their own drainage to the Pacific ocean. Those rivers which fall most immediately under the notice of actual settlers of the present day, are comprisd within the western division of Oregon. They are Willamet, the Umpqua and the Klamet, with their several tributaries. These rivers and their tributaries form valleys of moderate extent, and furnish many tolerable good farms to those who love a romantic life among the hills and vales of an undulating country. Wheat, oats, neat cattle and horses, are the principal sources of wealth which is derivd from the soil at present. Indian corn is not much cultivated in Oregon, its summers being too dry for corn to thrive well. The swine of the country look well fattend upon wheat, but the ox is mostly usd here for food.

I ought here to remark that the wheat of this country is of a superior quality. It is free from all those attending evils very common at the east, such as smut, rust and wheat sickness.—The weevil is not known here at present. The wheat of this country grows with a very stiff stalk, which enables it to stand erect for a great length of time. This furnishes the farmer during the dry season of the year an opportunity to secure his abundant crop.

The mineral resources of Oregon hitherto, have receivd but little attention. Gold has been discoverd only sparingly.—Copper is said to exist on the Cowlits, a small tributary to the Columbia river, on the north of it, having its source in the direction of Puget's sound.

Lead has of late been seen upon the Santyam. It is thought by some persons that it may be obtaind there in considerable quantities, but as the minds of the Oregon people are at present directed to the gold mines of California, little attention will be paid to mining operations at home. Iron exists in large quantities in the Cascade mountains. Along the emigrant route, I have seen iron probably as rich as 80 per cent.

The soil of the whole division west of the Cascade range is tingd of a reddish color by the red oxide of iron. This oxide in some places is so abundant as to injure the soil. In other places the soil is not materially injurd by it. In some places along the rocky bluffs of some of the rivers, iron ore is quite rich. I observd one of those places in the bluffs east of the Willamet falls, at the south end of Oregon city, where the road, leading to the top of the highest bluff is excavated. From my own observations in traveling over the western division, I am confident that there is no lack of iron ore in almost every part, and so soon as the inhabitants are ready to turn their attention to it, their necessary supplies will be furnishd from their own country.

The next subject relative to the Oregon country is its geological character. In remarking upon the geology of this country several departments of the science are presented to view. First, there are three ranges of mountains running nearly parallel with each other from north to south.

The eastern range which bounds the eastern side of Oregon, is along the dividing ridge of the American continent. If the question be asked, why this dividing ridge? the geologist alone attempts an answer. From the accumulation of facts hitherto adducd of the liquidity of the earth's interior, and the discharge for ages of its internal liquid matter upon the already formd crust, it is evident that its nucleus must become less than at first, and thereby produce a rigid and furrowd appearance of the crust, by its conforming through the power of gravitation to a lesser surface than that on which it was at first formd. Altho' isolated peaks of mountain ranges may be formd by accumulation of lava, and considerable districts may be raisd by the pressure of gasses from beneath, yet so considerable an elevation as the dividing ridge of the American continent can never be formd in such a way.

Oregon is truly an uneven and mountainous country. It is true that in passing from the dividing ridge westward, there are a few situations where the traveler views the country around him as apparently level, but this appearance continues on advancing along, but a short distance, till he is plunged into almost inextricable gulfs and deep ravines. The Blue mountains or intermediate range between the dividing ridge and the Cascade range, are of minor importance. They traverse no considerable extent of country, nor are they very wide. They have a volcanic appearance, and are strewd over with vescicular lava.

The Cascade range of mountains are more extensive, traversing by different names the whole of Oregon and California, at a distance of from 100 to 200 miles from the Pacific ocean. Some of its peaks are high and coverd with perpetual glaciers. This range, like the dividing ridge, seems to have been elevated by compression.

Between the Willamet valley and the ocean, is a range of high hills calld the Coast range. These are too rugged to admit of cultivation.

The western shore of Oregon is rocky, and in many places precipitous. If the theory that ocean beds are formd by undulations in the earth's crust be true, the query might arise, Why are ocean limits of precipitous rocks of the firmest material, as is the case with many of the ocean shores, and not a gradual slope from the land downward to the bed of the ocean? If it be admitted that rivers are formd by the expansive force of gasses acting beneath the earth's crust, it may be supposd that a fissure by similar means may be formd parallel and near to the shore of an ocean, so that its waters by their weight may produce a subsidence of that portion lying under them, whilst that part opposite the fissure remain stationary.

Oregon may be regarded as a primary country. Few fossiliferous rocks are seen in any part of it. I noticd on the west bank of Big Sandy creek, about thirty miles west of South pass, a few fossiliferous shale rocks. I have not noticd any in other places, though they may exist sparingly. From the American falls on Snake river, for several hundred miles westward the country is overlaid with a stratum of basaltic lava. This seems to be the true basalt, and although the rocks of the Willamet river at Oregon city have been considerd by some as basalt, from their extreme hardness, yet I have noticd that the surface of those rocks, after having been exposd to the weather, become a mere sand rock, by the loss of the iron with which they are impregnated. It is well known to mineralogists, that iron becomes soluble by the action of the atmosphere upon it, by which means water carries it from its parent bed to lower levels, where it is deposited, under the name of bog ore. The rocks at Oregon city consist of about three varieties of rock, differing not essentially in their properties, though some of them appear to have been subjected to so high a degree of heat as to render them somewhat crystaline or vitreous. The rocks at Oregon city are so fully impregnated with iron, that the magnetic needle, at some points along these rocks, is drawn aside from its polar position.

From what information I have obtaind in addition to my own observation respecting the rocks of Oregon, I am satisfied that few rocks except those of a silicious formation, exist here. Along the Columbia river, near its mouth, are a few lime rocks of inferior quality. At the Cascade falls, are whole trees of silicious petrefaction, showing distinctly the grains of the timber, and to what kind they belongd.

As the Willamet river has hitherto attracted the attention of actual settlers more than any other tributary of the Columbia river, I have concluded to give a more particular description of it than any other one belonging to the Western division of Oregon. From its confluence with the Columbia to the high country of its sources, the Willamet traverses a distance of about two hundred miles in extent. Its union with the Columbia is not much short of one hundred miles from the ocean. At the mouth of the Willamet, is a delta fifteen or twenty miles in length, calld Souvie's island, running nearly parallel with the Columbia. This island was formerly the residence of immense numbers of Indians. The Hudson Bay Company at present occupy it for farming purposes. At the eastern or upper mouth of the Willamet, are one or two other small deltas, though of no importance.

About fifteen miles from the Columbia, on the west bank of the Willamet, is a small town calld Portland. Ships of considerable burden visit this place for their lading.

Five miles farther up, on the east side, is a town newly laid out by Mr. Lot Whitcomb, calld Milwaukie. Vessels of considerable size can sail as far up as this place.

Seven or eight miles farther up, on the east side, is a tributary calld Clacamas. Its waters flow from the Cascade mountains. At the mouth of this tributary are rapids, which prevent ships from sailing up to Oregon city.

One mile farther up, is Oregon city on the east side, and Lynn city on the west side of the Willamet river. Between these two places is a bay, the waters of which are between three and four hundred feet deep. The width of the bay is about thirty rods, near the upper end at the crossing, and gradually widens downward to the Clackamas rapids.

Oregon city at present is built entirely upon the first terrace above the waters of the bay, and being so narrow that there is but one street that passes through the town lengthwise, excepting a Water street along the shore of the bay. East of the present town and contiguous to it, is a precipitous range of rocks, one hundred feet high from Main street, and so near to it that there is but just room enough for the accommodation of buildings with some very small gardens. On the top of this bluff, which is a second terrace from the waters of the river, the surveys for the town are extended, but no buildings have yet been erected there. Still back of this at a short distance, is a third terrace, elevated in hight equal to the surrounding country.

Oregon city is a new town, containing about 150 buildings, two saw mills, one of which is a double mill, and two grist mills. At each of these mills, water enough is wasted to carry four other mills. I think I may justly say, that there is water power enough at Oregon city to carry five hundred grist mills. It seems, on taking a view of the natural dam at the upper end of Oregon city, that when the fissure now constituting the river was formd, the paroxysmal effort from beneath causd a lateral dismemberment of some of the rocks along the sides of the fissure, and upon sliding down chokd up the chasm from one side to the other. Below the falls, the terrace on which the town stands seems to have taken a similar slide, but being filld in part with rubbish beneath, prevented an entire union of the rocks, leaving the chasm now constituting the bay.

The waters of the falls are precipitated over the cragged rocks at several different places, foaming and tumbling with tremendous roar, to the depth of thirty feet into the waters of the bay below.

About one mile and a half above the falls, on the west side of the river, is the small tributary calld Twality, issuing from the coast range.

Two or three miles farther up, is another slide of rocks, which chokes up the entire stream, with the exception of a small chasm or two, too narrow to admit boats of any considerable size to pass.

About twelve miles above Oregon city, on the east side of the river, Molala and Pudding river waters unite with the Willamet. These two tributaries have good supplies of water for mills. After having collected their waters from the hilly country east, they meander about over the land, and finally empty into the Willamet at one place.

About thirty miles above Oregon city, Yam creek unites with the Willamet, on its west side, watering the country from the coast range in two separate branches, till within about ten miles of the Willamet, where they unite and form one.

Salem, a small town on the east side of the Willamet, about forty-five miles above Oregon city, is the site of the missionary, Mr. Lee, of the Methodist order, now no more. At this place, is a classical school of considerable merit, the only one of importance in Oregon territory.

Rickreyall and Luckamute, on the west side of Willamet, contribute to its waters, but little above Salem.

Still farther up, and not more than eight or ten miles above Salem or the Institute as some call it, on the east side of the Willamet, is the Santyam, a stream of considerable importance, the principal branch of which flows from Mount Jefferson, one of the glacial peaks of the Cascade range. The course of this river from Mount Jefferson to its union with the Willamet, is not more than about forty miles.

Other tributaries of some importance still farther up, flow into the Willamet, on both sides of it, till arriving at the high country of their sources, where they ramify in all directions.

Leaving the subject of the Willamet river, I pass on to a description of the forests and animals of Oregon.

CHAPTER VIII

Forests and Animals of Oregon.

Between the South pass and the Blue mountains, across the Eastern division of Oregon, no forests encostume the earth, to emit their fragrant odors to cheer and exhilarate the weary and thirsty traveler, except on the Bear River mountains, a few isolated peaks scatterd over that barren region. Along the streams occasionally, however, are seen an inferior growth of timber and shrubbery of various kinds. The Blue mountains afford some dense clusters of timber of yellow pine, spruce-hemlock, and some fir. They do not, however, soar to the amazing hight of some of the trees of the Cascade mountains and the Western division. The Middle division is still more destitute of timber than the Eastern.

From the eastern side of the Cascade mountains westward to the Pacific ocean, the country is mostly coverd with timber. Many of the forests are so thickly set with under-brush, that they are with difficulty penetrated. Here, the fir is the most prevalent. Hemlock, cedar, soft or white maple as it is sometimes calld, oak and many other kinds of timber, are found in this division.

Timber of the same name with that of other countries, has a growth dissimilar. I have seen Laurel from one to two feet in diameter, and probably more than thirty feet high. Oak is generally inferior and scrubby. Hazel is sometimes from five to six inches in diameter, though it is commonly from one to two inches in diameter, being the only article of which hoops for barrels are made. Its hight is sometimes from twenty to twenty-five feet. Elder is often six inches in diameter, and from twenty to thirty feet high.

The largest tree I have seen in Oregon is a hemlock, standing near the shore of Young's bay, a little below the confluence of Young's with the Lewis and Clark's river, about two miles above their entrance into the Columbia, and about one mile and a half a little west of south from Astoria. This tree is about two hundred feet in hight, and measures, six feet from the ground, thirty-four and a half feet in circumference. The tallest tree that I have been enabld to measure, is in Oregon city. Its hight is about two hundred and seventy feet. I am, however, of opinion that taller timber may be seen at the foot of Laurel hill, in the Cascade mountains.

The trees of this country in many places are coverd with moss. I have noticd that the timber of evergreen countries is more commonly burdend with moss than those where defoliation is general. Hence, I am of opinion that Oregon will not be a very good country for fruit. I have observd that apple trees soon cover with moss, and appear of an inferior growth.

Among the native animals of this country, some of them are ferocious. The bear, tiger, panther and wolf, are of this class. The deer, the beaver and elk, are also natives of this country. The ferocious are sometimes known to attack the traveler, though it is not common. Those of the milder and gregarious classes obtain their support mostly from the bunch grass of the prairies.

It may here be remarkd, that no grass of this country, except along some of the river bottoms, grows in any other way than in the form of bunches, with intermediate spaces of several inches, and often of several feet.

CHAPTER IX

Magnetic Poles of the Earth—Variation of the Magnetic Needle—Phenomena of the Northern Lights.

Captain Ross, an English navigator, left England about twenty years ago, in pursuit of the north magnetical pole. He followd the magnetical needle, directing its course westwardly till he arrivd at Baffin's bay in America, where he left his ship and traveld about two hundred miles still farther west, at which place he determind to be the north magnetic pole. This point being several hundred miles south of the north geographical pole, determines its opposite or south magnetical pole to be an equal distance north of the south geographical pole, though on the opposite side of the earth.

From the north magnetic pole southward, the line of coincidence, or line of no variation as it is sometimes calld, passes through Hudson's bay, the state of Michigan, Ohio, and the several states lying south of these. This line forms a perfect circle around the earth, and the magnetic needle at any place on the earth within this circle will point directly through the magnetical poles coincident with the extreme points of the earth's geographical axis. The magnetic needle along this line is sometimes subject to slight vascillations, in consequence of the fluctuations of electricity occasiond by the heat of the sun, or geological differences of the earth's surface.

The variation of the magnetic needle in Oregon, among other things, has attracted my attention. Surveyors of this country tell me that the magnetical needle varies to the right of the geographical pole about 19 deg. and 20 min. Some, however, have observd in different places a variation of more than 20 degrees. This difference may be accounted for, by the great amount of iron disseminated through the country.

I have taken the trouble to draw a diagram of a section of the earth, to ascertain what the variation of the magnetic needle would be geometrically, at Oregon city. This corresponds, to a considerable degree of nearness, with experiments made with the compass. Concerning the depth to which the magnetic pole is seated in the earth, I have no means of ascertaining. This could best be done with a dipping needle along the line of no variation, at a suitable distance from the equator, so that the north end of the needle may have a perfect freedom of dip. Let the distance be ascertaind from the observer to the north magnetic pole, as manifested at the surface, which differs not much from two hundred miles, west of Baffin's bay. This distance may form the base line of a right-angled triangle. Let the surface angle at the magnetic pole be the right angle, and the dipping needle will show the angle at the place of the observer between the line on the surface of the earth and the line made by the dip. The observer then has a right-angled triangle, with sufficient data to ascertain at what depth the magnetic pole lies below the surface of the earth.

It would be gratifying to me, if some philosopher along the line of coincidence would take the trouble to ascertain the depth of the magnetic pole, and publish his experiments. Possibly, some day, a knowledge of that fact may add to the light of science.

The reasons why the magnetic needle at some places on the earth has a stationary variation from the geographical pole, and at others an annual movable variation, seems by some to be not easily accounted for, but I am of opinion that the same reasons may be assigned for the stationary position of the needle that are assigned for the stationary appearance of a planet in its orbit around the sun.

The motion of the magnetic pole around the earth, to an observer at any one point on the earth, as at London at present, presents during its whole circuit two stationary points or extremes to the left in its forward, and to the right in its retrograde movement. The extreme slowness of the magnetic pole round the earth, causes the stationary variation of the needle to remain nearly the same for a great many years. Hence so long as the magnetic pole continues to revolve around the earth, every other place on the earth will give in its turn a stationary and an annual variation.

Soon after my arrival at Oregon city, in the fall of the year, I observd that the central portion of that body of light calld Aurora Borealis, was as much to the right of the north geographical pole as the variation of the magnetic needle. I was then led to conclude that it was a constant attendant upon the north magnetical pole, moving westward gradually as the magnetic pole advances in that direction.

Very evidently the Northern Lights are occasiond by emissions of electrical light flowing from the great amount of electricity concentrated at the north magnetical pole.

CHAPTER X

Curiosities of Oregon.

It is difficult to tell, in making out a history of a country, what would be a curiosity and what would not, to readers that are familiar with descriptions of country scenery. I have selected a few that are considered by some as curiosities, as follows.

Mount Hood and its glacial sisters.

Bear Lake of Bear River.

Soda Springs.

Hot Springs.

Cascade Falls.

Mount Hood is one of the glacial peaks of the Cascade range of mountains. It is situated about 50 miles a little south of east from Oregon city, from whose vicinity it can be seen, and about 30 miles south of the Columbia river. Its height above tide water is about 11,721 feet. Rain seldom falls upon this mountain. Whenever it is enveloped by clouds, their contents are generally deposited in the form of snow. And in the summer season, the spectator from a neighboring mountain may frequently see it glistening with a brilliant white covering of snow, when only a few minutes before it had presented a mottled appearance of naked precipitous rocks, glacial prominences, huge caverns and deep ravines, so rapid is the passage of the clouds across the summit of this mountain. Alternately, during the summer season, the top of this mountain is coverd with clouds and then illuminated with a brilliant sun through a transparent sky. During the short season of repose from storms, the sun pours down its intense rays upon those snows and prominent glaciers, reducing them to water, which on its passage downward, especially in the hottest of the summer season, frequently deluges the whole base of the mountain, overturning and submerging to a considerable depth beneath rocks and sand bars, many of the most lofty and gigantic trees growing at the base and along the valley below.

On ascending this mountain, as the traveler arrives at the line of perpetual frost, he sees no verdure of any kind. Animals can only live to skirt across some of its lowest glaciers to other mountains more friendly to contribute to their support. Still advancing upward, the glaciers become more steep, till they with the walls of precipitous rocks, bid entire defiance to an ascension to the top of this interesting mountain.

In some of the lowest glaciers of Mount Hood are glacial caverns, several hundred feet deep, coverd from sight with sometimes only a thin covering of ice, with scarcely sufficient strength to sustain the weight of a man.

Mount Hood is a sample of the immense disintegrating power of glacio-aqueous agency. It cannot be expected that otherwise than great disintegrating power should exist where there are constant alternations of frost and water upon rock, as is the case upon Mount Hood. From this mountain flow several important streams of water, all of which, I believe, are constantly filled with a thick sediment of disintegrated rock.

Mount Hood on the east furnishes a considerable arm of Deshutes river. On the west, a large stream calld Sandy creek, and a part of Clackamas. Sandy, after a few miles of westerly course, runs north and falls into the Columbia river, a little below the Cascade falls. Another important stream calld Dog river, flows to the north and empties into the Columbia river above the Cascade falls. In fine, Mount Hood sits as queen of mountains within its vicinity, and being located centrally within that vast range of mountains, and elevated so much above all others as it is, must necessarily distribute its waters on all sides, breaking their way and bursting their barriers through other mountains of inferior size, till they are finally discharged into the ocean.

Mount Jefferson, another glacial peak, is situated centrally in the Cascade range of mountains, about 50 miles nearly south of Mount Hood, and about 40 miles east of the Willamet river. This glacier, as well as Mount Hood, contributes to the waters of Deshutes on the east, and the Willamet on the west. Its character is similar in most respects to Mount Hood, though somewhat inferior in size.

Mount St. Helen, on the north side of the Columbia river and about forty miles from it, is another high towring glacier of the Cascade range. This mountain, as seen from Oregon city, pierces the welkin high above the horizon around. Citizens of this country say that there are occasional emissions of smoke from its summit, though no lava of late has been seen flowing down its declivities. No successful attempt has been made to climb this mountain, to ascertain the size and appearance of its crater. It is the only one in this region that appears at present to show signs of volcanic activity.

Mount Rainier and Mt. Baker, still farther north along the Cascade range, are similar in character, less in size, and not very well known.

Bear lake and the Mineral springs are next to receive attention as curiosities.

Twelve or thirteen miles west of Thomas' fork of Bear river, is an extensive bottom of Bear river, where is a lake of unknown depth, and about three miles in width. Across this lake is a bar of earth, extending entirely from one bank to its opposite, rising about three feet above the waters of the lake, and wide enough for wagons to pass. This lake is a short distance above the confluence of its waters with Bear river. Its waters come from the mountains south of the lake, and are dischargd by percolation through this bar into the lake below it. From what I have seen of beaver dams in West Oregon, I am inclind to think this bar was made by those animals.

The Soda springs at Bear river, sixty-five miles east of Fort Hall, are considerd by some persons a curiosity. The bottoms of Bear river, at the springs and for several miles in extent along the emigrant route, appear to be cavernous. In the vicinity of the springs where most of them are located, emissions of gasses are observd from the surface of the land, and oftentimes with a considerable explosion. The springs likewise are constantly emitting gasses from them, as noticd by the bubbling of the water. The river at this place appears like a boiling pot.

The water of these springs is quite sedimentary. Numerous cones of silent springs are seen all around, occasiond by constant accumulations from the sediment of the waters. Some of the springs form craters or basin-shapd tops of several feet in diameter. These springs, after having been active a great number of years, choke up their orifices, and become silent. One which I saw on the bank of the river, calld by some the Steamboat spring, had nearly ceasd to flow. Its dying groans reminded me of a dying butcherd animal. Many of the springs are intermittent of a few seconds alternately. So soon as the gasses are sufficiently accumulated beneath, they are dischargd, often throwing the water to several feet.

Some of these springs are too alkaline to be pleasant to the taste, or even healthy. Others again, have a sufficient amount of acid in combination to render them tolerably pleasant. I believe, however, that none of them are as pleasant as the artificial soda of our shops.

About fifty miles east of Fort Boyce, along the south side of Snake river and near to it, are hot springs issuing from the plains. At their sources, they are scalding hot. Not far distant from these, on the north side of Snake river, are other similar springs. Fifteen or sixteen miles west of Fort Boyce, at the crossing of Malheur on the emigrant road, are other springs, some of which are so hot that a man cannot bear his hand in them two seconds. All of the hot springs are sulphurous.

From the volcanic character of a great portion of the country lying west of the dividing ridge of the American continent, it may probably be inferd that the water of these springs is heated by internal fires, not very deep-seated.

The Cascade falls are noticd by some travelers as worthy of attention. Some remarks relative to them may not be altogether uninteresting, as well also to correct some errors of former writers.

Mr. Eby, a late visitor of the falls, informd me that the country above the cascade is so nearly on a level with the country below, that were the rocks that choke up the river at the cascade removd, the water of the river would flow as smoothly and with as little apparent fall, as it does for miles above or below that place.

Immediately above the falls is an apparent subsidence of many acres of timberd land, so that the trees are standing in very deep water. But few of them at present remain. Visitors of the present day are of the opinion that the apparent subsidence is not one in reality, and that the place now submerged was once a bottom land, coverd with a dense growth of fir, and as the rocks precipitated from their stupendous columns into the river at that place, the waters were gradually damd up, so as to overflow the bottom of the river above.

The timber there submergd has become of a siliceous petrefaction, showing the grains of the timber as perfectly as if no such petrefaction had taken place.

After closing my remarks relative to the natural scenery of Oregon, I am led to suggest some ideas concerning the poor, degraded, primitive man of the country.

INDIANS OF OREGON

CHAPTER XI

Their Customs, Habits and Character.

The Indians of Oregon, notwithstanding the exertions that have been made to improve their condition, are still a degraded race of semi-human beings, rapidly approaching to total extinction. Such is the proneness of the human race to indolence and vice, that it requires the whole of a short life to make any considerable advances towards an improvement in his natural or mental condition, even amongst the most favord portions of the human family.

The Indian does not appear to have the most distant conceptions of any moral obligation towards another. He is prompted by tradition more than by a sense of duty, and the more he becomes enlightend, the more he becomes alive to vice.

The fox, taken from its lair in an infantile state, is only reard and shown to the lodgings of the domestic fowl of the barnyard, ere he escapes from the hands of his benefactor, with his prey, to his distant and secret abode, amongst the thicket of the forest. So the Indian. Point him to the comforts and enjoyments of a domestic life, and he looks upon them with indifference and disdain. Teach him that from the plow is derivd his food, and that in due time he may reap if he faint not, and yet if he is hungry he will resort to the potato patch of his neighbor and dig them all up so soon as they are planted, leaving his future well-being to the fates.

There is but little confidence reposd in each other respecting the safe-keeping of property, and it is impossible to make an Indian believe that it is morally wrong to steal. The only thing that prevents them from stealing, is the probability of being detected and punishd for it, and that Indian is smartest, who is keenest at the business.

At present, the few remaining Indians of Oregon are in a worse condition than before the whites settled amongst them. Formerly, they depended entirely on furs to keep them warm during the inclement season of the year, but now they are partly clad in skins and partly in garments nearly worn out, sold them by the whites for a trifling amount of labor, or such other pay as is agreed upon. With these, they are often amusingly and fantastically dressd. A man is sometimes seen wearing a bonnet, wrong side before. Sometimes a woman is seen wearing a man's shirt, and others, again, are seen wearing a dress, reversed. Sometimes, in the summer season, it would puzzle a Philadelphia lawyer to tell what kind of a dress they do wear, or whether — —

At present, there are probably not more than twenty-five Indians, who consider the Willamet valley their home, though others, from the upper country of the Columbia, resort to Oregon city to winter, because they can obtain support during that season more readily, where abundant supplies can be had at all times.

The mode of doctoring, when any prevalent disease is among them, has a tendency rapidly to depreciate their numbers. It is done by heating the system as hot as they can bear, in ovens made for that purpose, along the banks of streams, where the patient is shut in for several minutes, with heated pebbles, until he obtains a thorough sweat. He then rushes to the stream and plunges into the water, which cools the system so suddenly, that hundreds live to try the experiment but a few times.

Another depopulating mode of conduct is practicd amongst some of the tribes, which is that of flattening the head. The opinion that the Great Spirit can better distinguish between the aristocrat and his slave, in another world, has led to the practice of flattening the heads of the aristocracy, and leaving the heads of their slaves natural. This practice is common only amongst some of the tribes of the Western valley. Those Indians of the upper country, nominally Flat Heads, are so only in derision.

The mode of flattening the head, is to take the infant, at the first dawn of its existence, and lash firmly to its back a board, somewhat longer than the child and of suitable width, probably eight or ten inches, for it to lie upon when placd in a prostrate position. Its arms are brought downward to this board, and lashd so firmly that the infant cannot stir them. The board at its back reaches two or three inches above the head, so that the board which serves for flattening the head, being fastend to the top of this, is brought over the head forward to the edge of the brow. To the edges of this are fastend small cords, that are brought back and fastend to the board behind. These cords are drawn so tight that the board on the head forms an a acute angle at the top, with the board on its back. In this position, the miserable infant is kept more than three months, languishing for want of action. Sometimes, the blood gushes out from the nostrils and ears, from the severe pressure of the board.

But few survive the operation. When the operation is fully accomplishd, the head is flattend from the brow to the top of the head, though sometimes, in after life, it becomes a little raisd at the fontanelle and cross sutures.

An Indian can be taught to pray, and, in fact, they do often pray to their Tyee, or Big Spirit, as they call him, that he will give them a supply of venison and other present supplies—but what may be considerd a change of heart, is entirely foreign to an Indian.

A few years ago, at the station of Mr. Lee, upon the Willamet river, there was revival of religion, amongst whom were a considerable number of Indians. The whites succeeded in getting them to pray for awhile, but after they had prayd long enough, as they supposd, for a good lot of blankets, they began to call for them. The whites told them that they must not pray in that way. They replied, that they would not pray for them any more, if they would not pay them for what they had done.

The Indians at Dr. Whitman's station, on the Walla Walla river, have manifested, in their conduct towards him, what may truly be considerd traits of Indian character. Like a venomous serpent, that bites the hand that feeds it, so the Indians of that country, after incessant toil of ten or twelve years, to teach them husbandry and the various comforts of domestic life, stretchd forth their cruel hands, upon the 29th of November, 1847, and murdered himself and family.

I have long been of the opinion, that it is useless to send missionaries to barbarous races of men, for the sake of Christianizing them, or even civilizing them. The only benefit arising from an operation of that kind, is to furnish a foothold for the enterprising white man, who may follow the steps of the missionary, to seek a new home, where he may display his wisdom, in beautifying and improving the face of nature. Whom God has cursd, he is cursd, and whom God has blessd, truly is blessd.

Soon after the massacre of Dr. Whitman, the authorities of Oregon advisd all the missionaries of the upper country to leave their fields of operation, which they did, with the exception of Roman Catholics, who have some localities there.

It is difficult to determine what brought events to such a crisis as that of the death of Dr. Whitman. It is supposd by some, that the Roman Catholics sought an advantage to break up the Protestants at that place, by making the Indians believe that the whites were endeavoring to exterminate them, by introducing disease among them.

On their way to the Western valley of Oregon, some of the emigrants, who were afflicted with the measles, passd through Dr. Whitman's place, and imparted them to the Indians, from which cause, many of them died.

The Indians are great believers in sorcery. They are of the opinion, that the man who has power to cure, has also power to kill, by means of witchcraft. From this belief, has arisen the custom amongst the Indians, of killing their doctors, when any of their patients do not recover.

Before closing the subject of the Oregon Indians, I have seen fit to insert Mr. Spalding's account of Dr. Whitman's death, as given him by his own daughter, who was present during the distressing event, which is given by him as follows.

WAIILATPU MASSACRE

CHAPTER XII

Account of the murder of Dr. Whitman, as given by Rev. H. H. Spalding.

In this communication I will commence the history of the bloody tragedy of the 29th of November at Waiilatpu. In all such massacres there is usually one or more escapes to tell the dreadful tale. It would seem God rescued me from the murderer's hand, to perform this painful office. May kind Heaven grant that it may never again be my painful duty to record a like tragedy. May the friends of missions never again be calld upon to supply the places of their missionaries, cut down by the hands of those to whom they may be sent with the blessings of the gospel of peace. Especially may the dreadful act not again be done by the hands of those who have been baptized in the name of the sacred Trinity, and introducd into the Christian church. Considering all the circumstances which attended the massacre at Waiilatpu, I think it stands first on the catalogue of Indian crimes. The massacres committed in the first settlements of America, were the acts of uncivilized, unchristianizd heathens. The much lamented Dr. Whitman and esteemd lady and those who fell with them, were murderd by the Cayuse Indians, who wishd to be regarded a christianizd people, strictly honest, particularly friendly to the Americans, having adopted the habits of civilizd life—with whom my departed brother and sister had labord for more than eleven years, had been the means under God of introducing among them numerous herds of cattle, of planting fields of grain all through the country, had deliverd them from their former precarious source of subsistence roots and fish, and in their place, furnishd them, or causd them to possess in abundance, all the comforts of life, various grains, vegetables, milk, butter, beef, plows, &c. They had been indefatigable in their labors, to instruct them in the principles of the Christian religion and to introduce schools.

The Cayuse had become a praying people. In almost every lodge the family altar was erected. No doubt on the morning of the bloody 29th, the murderers were scrupulous to observe their morning devotions, again at evening, while the dead bodies of the slain lay about unburied, the food of the fowls of heaven and the beasts of the earth.

One of the actors of this horrible scene was a member of our church, and while he held one of the captives as his wife, the sport of his brutal passions, he was careful to have morning and evening prayer and to read a portion of scripture from his book, which we printed while he was in our school at Clear Water.

Their sick and dead had ever been the peculiar care and receivd the devoted attention of their missionaries. Yes my beloved associates, whose hands had so often furnishd winding sheets and coffins for their dead, were denied coffins and even a resting-place under the earth by this same professed Christian people. Such are the people who have committed the horrible murders of which it has become my painful duty to write.—Such the end of the once promising mission among the Cayuse Indians.

On the 18th of November Mr. Jackson, my daughter Eliza, ten years of age, and myself, left my place for Waiilatpu. My object was to spend a few weeks with Dr. Whitman, visiting his people, preaching, assisting him in his labors with the sick and dying. We were anxious to be present at some of the meetings which the Catholic priests were holding with the Indians to obtain locations near Waiilatpu, and to persuade the priests if possible, to allow the Indians to say whether Catholic or Protestant missionaries should remain among them. Should the Indians prefer the Catholic missionaries, we would then and ever been ready to leave the country and allow them to occupy the field unmolested. But should the Indians prefer that the Protestant missionaries should continue, we have ever felt the Catholics ought to leave us undisturbed. We have ever felt that unprotected by law, we could not be safe should the Catholics come into our field.

The feelings of the Indians were, that both missionaries could not occupy the same field. The Rev. Mr. Josette of the upper Catholic mission requested of the Nez Perces, two years ago, a location near my station. The principal chief Ellis said, "It will do for the French and English to have two religions, as they have laws, but for Indians who have no laws, it will not do. We have one religion with which we are satisfied. If the Catholics come in, there will be fighting immediately."

We have held ourselves ready to leave the country whenever the Indians as a body wishd it. Dr. Whitman twice during the last year calld the Cayuse together and told them if a majority wishd he would leave the country at once. The Cayuse chiefs unanimously said he must not leave, and among them were the principal persons who have staind their hands in his blood. Dr. W. held himself ready to sell the Waiilatpu station to the Catholic mission whenever a majority of the Cayuse might wish it, provided that mission might wish to purchase it and the other stations, and the mission might agree. I am not aware that the Catholic mission ever applied to Dr. Whitman to purchase the Waiilatpu station. However that may be, he would have proved recreant to the trust committed to him by the American Board, had he sold the station or left it unless desird by a majority of the people.

A few days before I arrivd at Waiilatpu, the bishop and his priests had held a meeting with the Cayuse at Walla-walla and laid before them again their wish to obtain a location near the doctor's station. Capt. Murray informs me that he was present at that meeting, and that Tamtsaky and Telapkaikt, said to the bishop, "That they would give him a station already furnishd with buildings, mills, fences, &c., that it was the one occupied by Dr. Whitman, that the doctor was a bad man and they were going to get rid of him." The bishop objected to taking the doctor's place. They then told him to come up and they would show him a place. Accordingly, the bishop or one of his priests did so, and a place was selected about four miles from the doctor's station.

On learning this, a Cayuse chief said to Telaukaikt, "Have you allowd the Catholic priest to select a location?" the answer was "Yes." The chief replied, with this strong language of rebuke, "Why did you not put the priest in the doctor's house at once?" that is, as understood by the Indians, "why did you not kill the doctor at once and give his property to the priests?" This last statement I receivd from my fallen brother the week before his death, who said, in view of this and other alarming movements of the Catholics, "Now if the Indians do not allow us to leave, my days are few, but if I am to fall by Catholic influence, I believe my death will do as much good for Oregon as my life can."

I arrivd at the station Nov. 22d. The doctor's large family had been sick with the measles, and three of the children were still dangerously ill. Mr. Osborn and his whole family were sick with the same disease. Many of the other white families at the station were just taking the measles. The Indians were sorely afflicted, dying every day, one, two, and sometimes five in a day, with the dysentery which very generally followd the measles. On the 24th Mr. Osborn's second child died. Mrs. Osborn and her youngest child continued very low.

As we are approaching the eve of the awful tragedy, I will here notice the white persons living at the station at the time of the massacre. The doctor's family consisted of himself and lady, Mr. Rogers, formerly our school teacher, now studying with a view to join our mission, Mr. and Miss Rewley, the former very sick at the time, seven orphan children of one family by the name of Sager, (father and mother died crossing the mountains in 1844,) the two daughters of Mr. Bridger and Mr. Meek, a half-breed Spanish boy, whom the doctor had brought up from infancy, and bound to the doctor by his father, and the two sons of Mr. Manson of the H. B. Co.

The following are the names of the families, their number and occupation, viz. Mr. Osborn millwright, Mrs. Osborn and three children, Mr. Camfield blacksmith, Mrs. Camfield and five children, Mr. Hall employd building store-houses for the Indians, Mrs. Hall and five children, Mr. Saunders school-teacher, Mrs. Saunders and five children, Mr. Marsh miller, one child, Mrs. Hayse and two children. At the saw-mill, twenty miles distant, Mr. Young mechanic, Mrs. Young, three sons young men, Mr. Smith cutting saw-logs, Mrs. Smith and five children, Mr. Hoffman employd in getting wheat for the Indians, Mr. Sails sick, Mr. Gillian tailor.

Most of these, contrary to the wish of the doctor, had stopd at the station to winter on account of weak teams or sickness. The doctor had been at considerable expense in exploring a new route from the Utilla to the Dalls, which avoided the sands and heavy hills of the Columbia river, led through good grass, and a nearer route. He was very solicitous to persuade as many of the emigration as possible to pass on to the Dalls, fearful that sickness and weak teams would compel more to stop at the station than he could procure provisions for. I had already packd over from my station, seventeen horse-loads of grain, expected to pack more, from time to time through the winter.

Very many who were persuaded to pass on to the lower country, felt rather hard at the doctor at the time, for not allowing them to stop. I thought myself he was over anxious. He is not to be blamd for the number of Americans that were wintering at his station, if any blame is to be attachd to this circumstance, but there is none, plainly because a number of Americans' wintering at Waiilatpu had nothing to do in bringing about the massacre. To insinuate otherwise, is a base slander upon the American character. That such insinuations, however, have gone forth, I am aware, but it is for no other purpose than to divert public attention from the true causes, and fasten it upon what was not the cause. If Americans were the cause, why were all the Americans killd? while the Catholics, down to the smallest child, were spard, caresd and permitted to dwell among the murderers to this day unharmed, and even now are commencing new stations among the Indians, while the last families of our American missionaries are being removd from the country by an escort from the army? The insinuation is as base and cruel as it is absurd.

There were also at the station three others who claimed to be Roman Catholics, names, Nicholas Finley, Joseph Stanfield, Jo Lewis. The two latter were in the employ of Dr. Whitman. Joseph Stanfield, a Canadian, had crossed the mountains in '46, had been in the employ of the doctor from that time. At his trial before Judge Wheeler two of the widows testified that Stanfield told them that he knew in the morning that the massacre was to take place that day. On being taken by the sheriff, he attempted to secrete a watch which belongd to one of the widows, also considerable money belonging to one of the murdered young men. Jo Lewis came into the country with the last emigration, at least from Fort Hall. Much uncertainty hangs about this individual. To the mission he claimd to be an Indian, born in Canada, of the Catholic faith, brought up in the state of Maine, had spent some time in California. Among the Indians he passd himself as a Chenook of the Catholic faith,—said that formerly the Americans (Protestants as understood in most instances of late by the word *Suyapu*) by ships brought poison to the lower country with a view to destroy all the Indians. Vast multitudes were destroyd, as their old men very well recollect—referring doubtless to the small-pox and measels which raged throughout the territory some 35 or 40 years ago. He, being a small child, was reserved by the Americans taken to the States, where he had grown up, ever mindful of his native country, and anxious to return to his own people. He told the Indians that he took particular notice of the letters of the Dr. and myself, from this country, told them that some of these letters spoke of this vast country every way desirable for settlements, its healthy climate, its rich soil, the bands of horses. Some of the letters calld for poisons by which we could sweep off the Indians, and make way for the Americans. In accordance with this request, he said, several bottles of poison had been brought over by the last emigration, which had caused many deaths among the immigrants, and was the cause of the sore sickness and frequent deaths among the Indians, and would soon kill them all if the Dr. and his lady and myself were not removd. This I receivd from Stikas in his lodge 24 hours after the butchery had taken place.

It seems that immediately on my arriving, Lewis set himself to excite the Indians to do the dreadful deed. He told them that he overheard the Dr. and myself consulting at night as to the most effectual way to kill off the Indians.

Such statements following like statements which have been sounding in our ears, and in the ears of Indians for years, and made with so much apparent solicitude for them, and at this time of great excitement among the Indians, on account of the measles, had doubtless much to do in bringing about the bloody tragedy. He took an active part in the murders—was seen by Mr. Camfield, from his place of retreat, to go up to the window in company with Tamtsaky, and beat them in, and soon after, to bring out goods.

Several times before Mrs. Whitman receivd her first wound, and after the doctor was senseless, Jo showd himself at the window with a gun in his hand. When Mrs. Whitman would speak to him, he would immediately go away. He brought the children down from the school room, and collected them in the kitchen, to be shot. When the chief gave orders not to shoot the children, and just as Mrs. Whitman was brought out upon the settee, where she receivd her mortal wounds, an Indian seizd Francis by the head, dragd him out from among the children, to the door of the Indian room, where Jo with his own hand, shot him.

The object of Lewis was doubtless plunder. Finley has a Cayuse, or Walla-walla wife, was campd near the doctor's. In his lodge, the murderers held their councils during the massacre, he being at the head. He partook of the plunder, and is said by the Nez Perces, to have considerable money. The part he took in the battles at the Utilla and the Tukanan, is better known to others than myself. He is now said to be in the Flat head country.

On the 23d, three Indians died, including a child. The Dr. as usual had coffins made for them, and winding sheets prepard and assistd in burying the dead. His visits to the sick and dying, were as frequent as the severe sickness in his and the other white families would allow. It was most distressing to go into a lodge of some ten fires, and count 20 or 25, some in the midst of measles, others in the last stages of dysentery, in the midst of every kind of filth, of itself sufficient to cause sickness, with no suitable means to alleviate their almost inconceivable sufferings, with perhaps one well person to look after the wants of two sick ones. Every where the sick and dying were pointed to Jesus, and the well were urgd to prepare for death.

24th. To day, a child of Mr. Osborn's died. We hopd that this affliction of Providence would show the Indians that the whites, in common with themselves, were exposd to the ravages of disease. But from the grave, Tintinmisi, a chief, followd us to the house, and repeatd to us, the old declaration,—"The Samh-Sismusismu, (black gowns,) every where tell us that you are causing us to die. I do not believe it myself, but some of the people do."

We told him that it was owing to cleanliness, and better nursing, that a less number of whites than Indians died—told them, (many were now collected,) if they listend to the false reports and drove us from the country, they would be a ruind people. But if they preferd the Catholic to the Protestant missions, let us know it, and we will leave the country immediately. They said we must not leave them.

CHAPTER XIII

Same subject continud.

25th. To-day, Mr. Jackson, Mr. Rogers and myself left for Walla-walla. Encampd with the Walla-walla chief, Piyu-piyu Maks-maks, (Yellow Swan, often calld Yellow Bird, or Yellow Serpent.) We had a pleasant interview. He said the Catholics had often urgd him to leave the Protestants, and join them, but he should never join them, as it was too much like their old religion, worshipping men, women, clothes, swords,—&c. They had frequently requestd of him a place for a station, but he had refused. They had told him in reply, he must go to hell, if he followd the Protestants. He replied that as you say the Protestants are bad, and I am bad, sure it is better that the bad go together. He said that they had frequently told him that we were poisoning the Indians, that the Bishop told them it was the Americans who brought the measles into the country, that God had sent this disease upon them, to show his displeasure at heretics.

This declaration, the chief thought the Bishops made in order to prejudice the Indians against the heretics. Immediately on its being made, the statement spread through the country like electricity. It was in the mouth of every Indian, old and young—the great chief of the Black gowns, (the Bishop,) tells us that the Americans brought the measles into the country—that God sends this disease among the heretics, to show the Indians how he hates the Americans. The excitement was intense, and we felt our situation to be most critical,—we felt that we were in danger from this source.

But the difficulties in our minds were, are these tangible evidences that we can present to the public and our Board, that will convince them that we are in danger from this source? Now that the bloody transaction has taken place, circumstances and facts seem to point so plainly to this source as the source whence originated the indirect causes of the massacre, that many are ready to exclaim, "why did you not leave your fields before?" And even our Catholic friends seem to be so thoroughly convincd that our situation was a dangerous one, that many of them are loudest in exclaiming, "you should have left your fields before." But so entirely hidden from the eye of the Christian world, were those influences we feard, that had we left 3 days before the massacre, the Papists would have settld quietly through the country, the Cayuse continued, as they have been for years, friendly to the Americans—had we publishd to the world as a reason of our leaving that we considerd our lives in danger from the influences which the Papists were every where exerting upon the minds of the Indians through their prejudices and superstitions, who would have believd us? The world, the church and the Board would have condemnd us as cowards leaving our work before there was danger.

Besides, the Board have ever enjoind upon us, as also the Captain of our salvation, to contend earnestly for the pure principles of christianity against the errors and subverting principles of Romanism, and NOT TO FLEE before them.

26th. Last night a niece of the chief died. He requested me to pray and converse with the afflicted family. He farther requested that after arriving at the fort, I would hold myself in readiness to attend the funeral as soon as the corpse could be taken to the fort some four miles distant, and preparations made for burying. As we were about to leave, the chief took me by the hand and said, his heart would ever be with the Americans. I am happy to learn that to a good degree, (considering the influences which have been about him,) he has kept his word.

Reachd the fort early. Found here the "Bishop of Walla-walla" and five priests. Three or four others had crossd to the north side of the Columbia river, and were commencing stations on the Yankmaw river. Let it be distinctly notied that this bishop was appointed "Bishop of Walla-walla," and sent into this field with his priests, while as yet there was not a Catholic church or station, or priest (stationary) in the whole district, but the field was entirely occupied by Protestant missionaries, most of whom had been quietly laboring in their places for eleven years.

Soon after we arrivd, a messenger came into the fort stating that all things were ready for the funeral services. Mr. Rogers accompanid me to the grave. A canoe had been cut into parts for the coffin and its cover.

On returning to the fort I enterd into familiar conversation with Rev. Mr. Brouette, one of the priests, who can speak very good English, on the subject of the "Catholic Ladder," which has, for several years, been distributed among our Indians, and I believe very generally through all the tribes of Oregon. This "Ladder" and the instructions which usually followd it, generally in the hands of half-breeds previously instructed, declard the Roman Catholic church to be the only true church—that the "Suyapu," [Protestants, Americans,] Heretics, had left the true church when Luther laid aside his black gown and cross and went after a maid,—that we were all going down to hell,—that while we Protestants by our poisons were causing them to die, by our instructions we were sending them to hell.

The excitement producd among the Indians by these measures was most intense. It is impossible for any one who was not a constant witness to conceive of the agitated state of the Indians when this alarm was fastend upon their superstitious minds, and consequently of our critical and dangerous situation. My attention had been suddenly arrested by the outcries and wailings of a whole camp, occasiond by the arrival of some one with an additional explanation of the "Catholic Ladder," always accompanied with the declaration, the American missions are causing us to die.

I told the priest that in self-defense and in order to counteract these false ideas, I had prepard a chart on which was exhibited the rise of the Papal church as predicted by Paul, 1st Timothy iv. 1-3, 2d Thes. ii. 3. I told him we understood where each other stood. He and his church regarded and pronouncd us vile heretics and worthy to be persecuted and expeld from the country, and reminded him of the means, the "Catholic Ladder," which would soon effect this object if not counteracted. On the other hand, we Protestants regarded the Papal church as the Man of Sin, and while I would as a neighbor afford them every facility my limited means would allow, to aid them in the beginning in the way of provisions, seeds, native books, &c., as I presumd they would do the same by us in like circumstances, as a minister of what I regarded the gospel of Christ, set for its defense in this part of the world, and especially as having been first and long in the field, we should exert ourselves to the utmost to enlighten and instruct the people, to disabuse them of the errors and highly inflammatory doctrines every where spreading through the country by this "Catholic Ladder" and its teachers, greatly to our prejudice and danger.

Not to do any thing like working behind their backs, the chart was brought and spread out before the bishop and his priests, and briefly explaind.

The equality of the apostles as declard by their great Head, is exhibited on this chart. The rise of the Man of Sin as foretold by Paul, and which history and observation compel us to believe to be the church of Rome by one markd sign, "forbidding to marry," and the abominable sin of idolatry in the worship of many and the bowing to the cross—is represented in the chart, sitting in the temple of God, proclaiming himself to be God, by the act of expiating given sins for fixd sums of money, as 10s 6d for killing a father, brother or wife, 18s for going into a nunnery alone, &c., and the burning of Bibles in New York in 1843, are represented. Other abominations as substantiated by history and Catholic authors, are shown.

The exhibition of this chart calld forth a close but friendly discussion. I askd one question—Is it true as claimd by one of your authors that the priest has the power to reproduce the person of the Lord Jesus Christ? Mr. Brouette replied distinctly, that he and every priest had power given them to recreate the person of Jesus Christ entire, flesh, bones, blood, head, hands, feet, &c., just as he was while on earth, and farther, they have the power to communicate the Holy Ghost, and to give even the Father himself. My blood ran cold! I was shockd at the horrible blasphemy of my friend, who otherwise treated me like a gentleman.

I told him if I could be made to believe that I had the power to reproduce the person of Christ our Lord, I should be horribly shockd at the idea of taking the deadly weapon and of committing murder, and of cutting up this body and feeding it to the people, and so convert them into a herd of cannibals, which is repeated many times every day in the Roman Catholic church in the mass. He replied that it was the glorified body of the Lord that they reproducd and sacrificd, and therefore it could not be susceptible of suffering when cut up. I replied, your mass then answers no purpose. The law of God requires as a condition of salvation, "without shedding of blood," i. e. without suffering, "there is no remission of sins." The glorified body of Christ cannot shed blood or suffer. He then shifted back again and said, we continue the sacrifice that was commencd on the cross. I rejoind, you admit the awful fact. The natural, real person of our blessed Saviour was naild to the cross and murderd by the wicked Jews. You claim to continue that murder. Therefore by your own positions you are murderers and cannibals,—therefore it follows unavoidably that the system of Catholicism is downright cannibalism or base deception.

After tea, to which Mr. McRean kindly invited us, in company with the bishop and his priests, our party left for Waiilatpu. Encampd on the Tushee.

27th. Arrived at the station early. A message had arrivd from Hezekich or Five Crows, and Tauwitwai on the Utilla, soliciting Dr. Whitman to visit the sick in that camp. I should have mentiond under date of 25th, that a Nez Perces in the camp of the Walla-walla chief, came to our tent and askd if the doctor was not killd, with as much indifference as if he had been inquiring about a horse. I replied, no. He said he heard the doctor was to be killd. This Nez Perce was a young man from my place, in whose statements no one ever expects to place any confidence. Had he been apprizd of the purpose of the Cayuse to destroy all Americans, I think he would have apprizd Mr. Jackson and myself, being our particular friend.

I stated this to the doctor, Mr. Kimble and others, at the station,—we considerd it a re-iteration of what had been said for a long time, "A ball can penetrate your body." True it was a time of great excitement among the people on account of the measles and dysentery which they every where said the Catholic priests told them were causd by us.

The doctor in one of his visits to the sick, had discovered Tamahas, (calld the murderer for having killd several Indians, who had just before lost his wife and who was the person, that, afterwards with two blows upon the head, laid our lamented brother bleeding, senseless but not lifeless, upon the floor,) in rather a suspicious attitude. From that time, the doctor had been cautious. But there were no inflammatory meetings among the chiefs as there had often been. For instance, when they returnd from California two years ago after the death of the son of the Walla-walla chief, several meetings were held to consider whether the doctor, myself or some other American teacher, should be killd as a set-off for Elijah. They came to the conclusion of a great majority at least, and I believe unanimous, that no one should be killd, and pledgd themselves in a full meeting, at which all those principal persons who have staind their hands in the blood of their teachers, as also the doctor and myself, were present, that we should not be injurd, and said we must not leave the country.

Again, when a party of Nez Perces returnd from the Catholic station among the Pointed-hearts, for many days fiery meetings were held through the camp, at which were re-iterated like a lesson well learnd, what they declard one and all they had receivd from the priests at the station, (in which were insinuations and assertions that endangerd our lives,) we were the authors of their sickness and death, the teachers of doctrines which would ruin the Indians. But now there were none of these meetings. On the other hand, all the Indians appeard friendly, were constantly coming for medicines, gruels, and other food, and warm in expressing their gratitude to the doctor for his unwearied labors among them.

The Cayuse at this time were in a more promising attitude than ever before. They were enlarging their farms, fencing them better, employing the doctor to build granaries, break up land, build fences, &c., who kept from time to time several teams employd in this business. Their attention to religious instruction was not abated. They were giving the doctor no trouble as formerly, about the mills, the land, the timber, &c. In fact, aside from the fearful movements of the Catholics crowding in upon us, the doctor was more encouragd than at any time before.

If any are disposd to attach blame to Dr. Whitman because he did not arm himself and others on that day and prepare for defense, let that blame rest upon the living,—let it rest upon the writer, and not upon the eminently devoted, pious and highly useful missionary whose name with that of his worthy companion I love to cherish, but whose death I am compeld to record—whose name I know every friend of the red man, as also every true American, will love to hand down to the coming generation, as the name of an eminently devoted missionary and warm-hearted friend of his suffering countrymen, immigrating to this country.

I know that one in high authority in the Catholic church, in a late publication, by a well meant and well studied silence, would give a very different character to my departed brother, as also more than intimate that the first Christian effort is yet to be made to civilize and Christianize the Cayuse and Nez Perce Indians. The design of the reverend gentleman in hanging out his colors so soon, was doubtless, that his people might know where he stood. I am greatly mistaken if there are not others who will read a lesson upon those colors. But we must expect such things from such hands,—hands which are uplifted not against the Protestant religion only, but against our dearest, noblest, immortal American temple, as can be shown from their attempting to annihilate the civil institution of marriage.

But there is no blame to be attachd to any for neglecting to arm ourselves. The doctor had not a load of ammunition in his house,—the immigrants living at the station had ammunition, and I think the doctor's boys had a few loads. Suppose the doctor had made an attempt to arm and defend himself,—the attempt would have been known and rousd the Indians. Besides, Jo Lewis was in the doctor's family, and apparently his best friend. He would have been among the first armd for defense—and what a defense it would have been!

The doctor requested me to accompany him to the Utilla. Leaving dear sister Whitman for the last time in this world, greatly exhausted by her long and incessant watchings and labors with the sick, with three of her children and one of Mr. Osborn's yet dangerously ill, to require her constant attention, Mrs. Osborn not yet able to leave her bed, and leaving my daughter—oh horrible!—to fall a captive into the hands of murderers, the doctor and myself started about sun-down.

CHAPTER XIV

Same subject continud.

The Utilla is about 20 miles from Waiilatpu, prairie country, as is the whole of the middle district of Oregon, with the exception of one or two mountains, at intervals of one and two hundred miles.

The night was dark, and the rain and wind beat furiously upon us. But our interview was sweet. We little thought it was to be our last. With feelings of deepest emotion, we calld to mind, that eleven years before, we crossd this trail the day before we reachd Walla-walla, the end of our seven months' journey from New York. We little thought the journey of life was so soon to close. We calld to mind the high hopes and thrilling interests which had been awakend during the year that followd—of our successful labors, and the constant devotedness of the Indians to improvement. True, we rememberd the months of deep solicitude we had had, occasiond by the increasing, menacing demands of the Indians for pay for their water, their wood, their air, their lands. But much of this had passd away, and the Cayuse, as to efforts for improvement, and menacing the station, were in a far more encouraging condition than ever before.

But the principal topic of conversation during that dark night was the danger that threatend from another source. The little cloud, as a man's hand, which had been hanging for some years in the distant horizon, now assumd a darker and more alarming appearance. The Papal Bishop and his priests seemd determind to crowd themselves upon us, and without consultation.

We felt that the present sickness among the Indians afforded the Catholics a favorable opportunity to excite the Indians to drive us from the country. And all the movements seemd to indicate that this would soon be attempted if not executed. Besides, we are informd by their own writers, that the oath of every priest requires him to oppose, to persecute and to ruinate every heretic, and every other power, but the Papal power, to the utmost of his ability. But my worthy brother replied, "in God we put our trust," and repeated "if I am to fall by Roman Catholic influence, I believe my death will do as much good to Oregon as my life can."

We arrivd late at the lodge of Stickas, thoroughly wet. In coming down the hill to the lodge, my horse fell and rolld partly over me, which causd severe pains in the head, and one leg, through the night and the next day. We spread down our blankets by a good fire in the lodge, and lay till morning.

28—Sabbath. Stackas, after family worship, prepard for us a good breakfast of potatoes, squash, fresh beef, and wheatbread of his wife's make. My departed brother observd how gratifying to notice the advancement of this people—their present abundant means for comfortable living, compard with their wretchedness and starvation, when we arrivd among them ten years ago.

I was particularly struck with the stillness and the order that prevaild in the lodge, and through the village, during the Sabbath.

The Dr. was immediately sent for, and after breakfast, he went over the river, to visit the sick, in the villages of Tawitwai, Pa-hat-ko-ko, (Five crows, Yumhawalis, (Growling bear.) At the hour appointed, the Indians were collected, and I explain to them the way of salvation.

About 4 o'clock, the Dr. returnd much fatigued, but said the sickness in his family, made it his duty to return home—said he had taken tea with the Bishop and two of his priests, who had arrivd from Walla-walla, the night before, and were occupying a house belonging to Tawitwai, (young chief,) built for him some years ago, by Mr. Pambran—said he had invited the Bishop and his priests to visit him, which they promisd to do in a short time. The doctor was much pleasd with the idea—hoping that we might come to some understanding and bring it before the people, to say who should be their missionaries.—I consented to remain, visit the sick and dying, and preach to the people a few days, then take my daughter and return home. Mr. Rogers expected to return home with us, to give his undivided attention to the native language. My dear brother bade me good evening, and left about sundown, although he greatly needed sleep and rest. My eyes saw him for the last time, as he passd at good speed over the hill, in the distance—to fall with his dear companion, at their post of duty.

What follows, I have receivd from the children, widows and others, who escapd the bloody massacre. I have taken every precaution, and made extensive inquiries, and believe the statement can be relied on.

Our devoted friend reachd home at 12 at night, and after examining the sick, took some rest. In the morning, he was at his work, administering to the sick, in the families of the whites and the Indians. That night or morning, an Indian died. The doctor as usual, had a coffin and winding sheet prepard, and assisted the friends in burying. He observd, on returning to the house, that but two or three attended at the grave.

As the doctor returnd from the grave, great numbers of Indians were observd gathering about the station, but an ox had been killd, and was being dressd, and was supposd to be the cause, as the Indians on such occasions, always collect in great numbers, and often from a distance.

Joseph Stanfield had brought in the ox from the plains, — which had been shot by Francis. Messrs. Kimble, Camfield, and Hoffman, were dressing the beef between the two houses. Mr. Saunders was in the school which he had just calld in for the afternoon. Mr. Marsh was grinding at the mill. Mr. Gillan was upon his tutor's bench, in the large adobie house, calld the mansion, a short distance from the dwelling of the doctor, — Mr. Hull was at work, laying a floor to a room adjoining the doctor's house. Mr. Rogers was in the garden. Mr. Osborn and family were in the Indian room adjoining the doctors seting room. Young Mr. Sails was sick in the family of Mr. Camfield, who were living in the blacksmith's shop. Young Mr. Bewley was sick in the doctor's house. John Sager was sitting in the kitchen, but partially recoverd from the measles. — The doctor and his lady, with their three sick children and a sick child of Mr. Osborn, and Mrs. Osborn, were sitting in the dining or sitting room. Several Indians came to the middle door, and requested the Doctor to come into the kitchen. He did so, shutting the door after him, and taking the Bible in which he was reading, and which I believe is now in the hands of one who escapd, and having upon it the marks of blood. — Edward sat down by his side, and was earnestly soliciting medicines, while Tamahas, an Indian calld the murderer, came behind him, and drawing a pipe-tomahawk from under his blanket, struck the doctor in the back of the head. The first blow only stunnd him, and his head fell upon his breast, but a second, which followd instantly upon the top of his head, brought him senseless but not lifeless upon the floor. John, rising up, attempted to draw a pistol. The Indians before him, rushd to the door, crying out, "he will shoot us," but those behind, seizd his arm, and he was thrown upon the floor. At the same instant, he receivd several shots from every direction, while a number with tomahawks and knives, rushd upon him, and cut him terribly to pieces. His throat was cut, and a woollen tippet stuck into it. Still he lingerd. In the struggle, two Indians were wounded, one in the foot, and one in the hand, by each other.

As soon as the tumult commencd, Mrs. Whitman, overhearing, and judging the cause, commencd in agony, to stamp upon the floor, and wring her hands crying out, "oh the Indians! the Indians! that Jo has done it all!"

Mrs. Osborn stepd into her room with her child, and in a short time, Mr. Osborn and family were secreted under the floor.

Without coming into the other rooms, the Indians left the kitchen, doubtless to aid in the dreadful work without. At this moment, Mrs. Hayse ran in from the Mansion, and with her assistance, Mrs. Whitman drew her dying husband into the dining room, and placing his mangled, bleeding head upon a pillow, and did all her frightful situation would allow, to stay the blood, and revive her husband, but to no purpose—the dreadful work was done. To every question that was put to him, he would simply reply "no," in a low whisper.

Probably after he receivd the first blow, he was not sensible of his situation. About this time, Mr. Kimble, from the beef, ran into the room through the kitchen, and rushd up stairs with a broken arm hanging by his side. He was followd immediately by Mr. Rogers, who in addition to a broken arm, was tomahawkd in the side of the head, and coverd with blood. He assisted Mrs. Whitman, in making fast all the doors, and in removing the sick children up stairs. Jo Lewis was seen several times approaching one of the windows with a gun, but when Mrs. W. would ask, "Jo, what do you want?" he would flee away.

By this time, the scene without had reachd the summit of its fury. The screams of the fleeing, fainting women and children—the groans and struggles of the failing, dying victims—the roar of the musketry—the clash of war clubs,—the whistling of balls—the clouds of burning powder,—the furious riding and rushing of naked, painted Indians,—the unearthly yells of infuriated savages, self-maddend, like tigers, by the smell of human blood,—all, all, require other language, and other ears than those of civilized beings! My blood chills as I write. But I am amazd at the self possession of dear Mrs. Whitman. In the midst of the terrible scene, she leaves not the room of her pale, gasping husband. Two Americans were overpowerd by crowds of savages, and hewd down by her window. It attractted her attention but for a moment—but this afforded an opportunity for a young Indian, who had always been particularly favord by Mrs. Whitman, to level his gun. His victim receivd the ball through the window in her right breast, and fell, uttering a single groan. In a few moments, she revivd, rose and went to the settee, kneeld in prayer. She was heard to pray for her dear children, now to be left orphans a second time, and that her aged father and mother might be sustaind under the terrible shock, which the news of her fate must occasion.

Soon after this, faint and bleeding, she was helpd into the chamber, where were now collected Mrs. Whitman, Mrs. Kimble, Mr. Rogers, all wounded and fainting with the loss of blood—Mr. Hayse, Mrs. Bewley, Catharine Sager, 13 years of age, and the three sick children.

They had scarcely gaind this temporary retreat, when the crash of the windows and doors, the deafening war whoop took the last hope from their fainting bosoms.

The under rooms were plunderd of all their property, the furniture dashd to pieces, and cast out. Jo Lewis was seen among the foremost to dash in the windows and bring out the goods. Here a deed was perpetrated, that exhibits the deep treachery and malignity of the Indian character—

Telaukaikt came into the room, where the doctor lay yet breathing, and with his hatchet, deliberately chopd his face terribly to pieces, but still left him alive.

Telaukaikt was a principal chief, had ever receivd markd favors from the doctor. A store house was then about being completed for him by the doctor. For several years he had exhibited a good christian character, and was on probation for admission into the church. But such was the return for untold favors, and such the end of his religion. A few days before, it will be recollected, he had given a piece of land to the priests, to commence a mission station within 4 miles of the Dr.'s house and told the Bishop they were going to get rid of the Doctor—according to Capt. McKay's statement. The same hatchet or some other, cut several deep gashes in the face of John, while he was yet living.

About this time, Jo Lewis went up into the school room and sought out the children, who were hid in the upper loft, and brought them into the kitchen to be shot.

CHAPTER XV

The same subject continud.

As Francis passd by his mangled, gasping brother, he stoopd and took the woollen tippet from the gash in the throat, when John attempted to speak, but immediately expired. Upon this Francis turnd to his sisters, and said, "I shall soon follow my brother."

The children were kept in this indescribably painful attitude for some time. My daughter Eliza was among them and understood every word of the Indians, who having finishd their terrible work without, were filling the room and the doors with their guns pointed at the hearts and heads of the children, and constantly yelling, "shall we shoot now?"

Eliza says her blood became cold, and she could not stand, but leand over upon the sink, covering her face with her apron that she might not see them shoot her.

Oh what pen can depict the feelings of these lambs? From this place, they were removd out of the door, by the side of the Indian room, just before Mrs. Whitman was brought out to be shot.

Immediately on breaking into the house, the Indians calld to Mrs. Whitman and Mr. Rogers to come down, but on reciving no answer, Tamtsaky started to go up stairs, but discovering the end of an old gun, which was laid over the head of the stairs, he desisted, and enterd into conversation with those above. He urgd them to come down, assuring them that no one should be hurt. Mrs. Whitman told him she was shot—and had not strength to come down, besides, she feard they would kill her. Tamtsaky expressd much sorrow that she was wounded, and promisd that no one should be hurt, if they wo'd come down. Mrs. W. replied, "if you are my friend, come up and see me." He objected, saying there were Americans hid in the chamber, with arms to kill him. Mr. Rogers, standing at the head of the stairs, assured him there were none, and very soon, he went up stairs, and remaind some time, apparently sympathizing with the sufferers, addressing them in the softest words, assuring them that he was heartily sorry for what had taken place, and advisd and urgd Mrs. Whitman to go down and be taken over to the other house, where the families were, and left them by assuring them that they should not be hurt if they would go down, intimating that the young men would destroy the house that night. About this time, the cry was heard, "we will now burn," "we will now burn."

There was no alternative. A terrible death by fire, in which all the children and the sick in the house, would be involvd, or that Mrs. Whitman and Mr. Rogers should throw themselves upon the promise of Tamtsaky. They chose the latter, as every one would, and our dear, devoted sister, leaning upon the arm of our dear brother Rogers, both faint with the loss of blood, stepd forth from the chamber, to be——! Oh,—my pen, speak not till forcd to name the awful deed!

Mrs. Hayse followd to assist Mrs. Whitman, who on reaching the lower room was laid upon a settee close by her yet dying husband. But oh how changd! that belovd face, the home of her earthly felicity, she had a short time before washd with her tears, and left it white with the paleness of death, now horribly cut to pieces, the upper part hanging over the chin, but gasping for breath. The sight was too much and she calld for air. Our dear brother was not seen to breathe after this, altho' he might have lingerd some time, as darkness soon set in. The settee was borne by Mr. Rogers and Mrs. Hayse out of the sitting-room, through the kitchen, over the mangld body of John, through crowds of Indians and out of the door towards the Indian room where the children were collected. Just as the settee passd out of the door, the word was given by the chief not to shoot the children.

At this moment Mr. Rogers, discovering their treachery, had only time to drop the settee, and raising his hands, exclaimd, "Oh my God," when a volley of guns were fird from within and without the house, a part at sister Whitman and a part at brother Rogers, and he fell upon his face, piercd with many balls. Sister Whitman was shot in several places, lying upon the settee. Balls flew in every direction, striking the walls by the sides of the children. My daughter says the guns were so near her head that the flashes burnt her hair, and the burning powder mingled with human gore seemd ready to suffocate them. But there was no escape.

At this moment an Indian seizd Francis by the head, and dragd him a few steps from the children, where Jo Lewis, drawing a pistol, cried out "you bad boy," and dischargd the contents into the lower part of his throat, and laid him bleeding at the feet of the other children, who expected every moment to mingle their bodies in the mud and blood with their groaning, dying mother and brothers.

The scene that follows beggars description and hurls us back amid the darkest days of Indian atrocity and savage cruelty. A savage seizd the blanket upon which the suffering Mrs. Whitman lay, and hurld her groaning and struggling into the mud. The brutal hand that gave her the first wound through the window, now seizd her by the hair of the head, crying out "you bad woman," gave her several blows in the face with his whip, amid the deafning yells, the shouts and the dancing of crowds of women and children and men, who seemd to vie with each other in pouring the greatest possible amount of suffering and pain into the bosoms of their dying victims. Some attempted to force their horses over the bodies, while others with whips or clubs seemd to take fiendish delight in beating their faces every time they struggld or groand.

The night came on and removd the savage demons from this scene of torturing, to the house where the captive women and children were collecting to become for weeks the sport of their brutal passions, the victims of their savage cruelties. But these bleeding, suffering lambs of Christ, although piercd with many balls and horribly beaten, lingerd on till in the night. Their dying groans were distinctly heard by Mrs. Osborn. The voice of Mrs. Whitman and Francis died away about the same time, soon after dark. But Mr. Rogers continud longer, his voice becoming fainter. His last words were, "come Lord Jesus, come quickly." Soon after this, Mr. Osborn and family left the Indian room, and passd on partly over the body of Francis which appeard to be lifeless. And it is hopd that very soon after their voices ceasd, these victims of savage cruelties found themselves at rest sweetly in the bosom of the Saviour, their labors, their fears, their pains ended, and their joys, unending joys, begun.

Mr. Kimble with the three sick children, also Catharine and I believe Miss Bewley, continud in the chamber through the night. Catharine tore up a sheet and bound up the broken arm of Mr. Kimble. After Francis was shot, and while the multitude were engagd in feasting their fiendish passions on the dying agonies of Mr. Rogers, Mrs. Whitman and Francis, Ups, Moolpool, (Walla-walla Indians in the employ of the doctor,) collected the other children in the buttery and attempted to comfort them. About dark they were taken over to the Mansion.

The first firing commencd at half-past one. Brother Rogers and sister Whitman left the chamber about sundown.

It appears the attack was simultaneous upon the different points. Mr. Gillan was shot upon his bench, the ball entering his breast and coming out at his back. He was assisted by Mrs. Saunders into another room, and expird about midnight. Mr. Marsh was shot at the mill, ran a little distance in the direction of the doctor's house, and fell. Mr. Saunders, hearing the guns, rushd to the door of the school-room, where he was seizd by several Indians who threw him upon the ground amid a shower of balls and tomahawks. Being a very active man, he gaind his feet and ran in the direction of his house, and although he was thrown down several times and doubtless receivd many wounds, he gaind the end of the field near the mansion some twenty rods from the school-room, when overpowerd by numbers, he fell to rise no more.

Mr. Hall was seen struggling with a single Indian for a gun which had missd fire — he wrenchd it from the Indian and rushd to the bushes wounded in the face, and during the afternoon and night found his way to Walla-walla, 25 miles distant. It appears from Mr. Osborn's statement, that Mr. Hall remaind at Walla-walla during Tuesday, determind not to leave, but hearing the women and children were slaughterd, in despair he consented to be put over the river at night, and started for the lower country.

This corresponds with the statement which the Indians said was given to them at the fort, and reachd my place by a Nez Perce, the next Monday, the day before I arrivd at home. I know it has been publishd that he could not be persuaded to remain. But is it natural to suppose a man would willingly leave a fort well armd and defended, and expose himself for three hundred miles through a country swarming with savages who murderd his countrymen, and from whose hands he had barely escapd? Mr. Hall never reachd the settlements. Indian report says he was murderd by the Indians in the vicinity of John Day's river. Another report says he was drownd in the Columbia river while attempting to pass a rapid in a canoe. The three men at the beef found themselves suddenly in the midst of a storm of balls and flaming powder, dischargd from a forest of muskets and pistols at their very bosoms. All three were wounded, but neither of them fell. They fled each as he could see an opening through the crowds. Mr. Kimble with a broken arm rushd into the doctor's house and chamber as stated above. Mr. Camfield ran by the blacksmith shop, seizd his youngest child and calld to his family to follow him. They ran into the mansion, and he rushd into the chamber, and from a small window had a clear view of the awful scene without. Mr. Saunders was about being cut down. Mr. Hoffman was yet falling and rising and struggling with overpowering numbers, in the midst of clowds of burning powder, the roar of guns, the clash of war-clubs, and the screams and yells of the savages. He had first taken the direction of the mill, defending himself with a single knife. The crowd was now making toward the house and he in the midst, when two horsemen having finishd their work at some other point, with tomahawks streaming with blood rushd upon him, and he fell, literally cut to pieces. He was cut open through the back, and his heart and liver taken out and found by his side on the ground, by my daughter, two days after, who replacd them and sewd a sheet around the body before it was, with the others, taken to the pit.

Neither of the Catholics were in any way molested. Jo Lewis was one with the murderers. Finley's lodge was near the mill, where the murderers held frequent councils during the massacre. Jo Stanfield was told by Telaukait to put his property by itself, that the Indians might know what was his and not molest it. He was seen to pass among the Indians as tho' nothing was going on. He told three of the women, two of whose husbands were slain, that he knew the murder was going to take place before he went after the beef, as appears from their testimony before Judge Wheeler. He told the widow Hayse that day, if she would become his wife the Indians would not molest her.

When the massacre commencd, the two sons of Mr. Manson, and David, the doctor's half-breed Spanish boy some nine years old, were separated from the other school children, and taken to Finley's lodge, whence they were taken to Fort Walla-walla. The selecting of David from the other children in the doctor's family, was a nice distinction, and could not have happend by chance. Two other half-breed children were left, but their fathers were Americans. David's father was a Catholic, but his mother was an Indian woman, who when her child was young, had cast it into a pit and left it to die. The doctor learning the fact, went to the place, took out the child and adopted it as his own, had educated and bestowd much labor and care upon the child, and he had become a promising boy. His father before his death had bound him to the doctor. I am sorry to say the boy is retaind at Walla-walla, probably by the priests, notwithstanding my remonstrance. As well might any other of the doctor's children have been retaind.

Mr. Camfield remaind in the chamber till some time after dark, when the Indians became quiet. He furnishd himself with a buffalo robe and some provisions and bid farewell to his family, not daring to hope that they might ever again meet in this world. He could be of no service to them by remaining and exposing his life, which would be taken the moment one of the murderers should discover him.

As yet none of the male children and none of the women but Mrs. Whitman had been killd, and the chief Telaukaikt had said they should not be injurd. True there was but a faint hope that Mr. C. could escape from the Indian country to a place of safety. But the most hazardous undertaking is cheerfully espousd when life is at stake. Mr. C. took the direction of my place, although a perfect stranger to the country and the route. He went some four miles and secreted himself in the brush to await a horse which

Stanfield was to bring to him the next morning if he could do it unobservd. He remaind secreted most of the day (Tuesday)—saw Indians pass near and heard several guns in the direction of the station, and of course had the most intense fears for the women and children.

As I was expected from the Utilla that day, he supposd that I had very probably fallen. But the victims were Mr. Kimble and the young Mr. Young,—the latter had come down from the saw-mill with lumber and was to return immediately with provisions for the families. He had arrivd within half a mile of the house, when the Indians met and shot him about 2 P. M.—about the time the priest arrivd in the camp. The team was turnd loose except one ox which attempted to hook and was shot.

Mr. Kimble remaind in the chamber through the night, suffering the most excruciating pain from his broken arm, still more distress of soul from the cries and moaning of the 3 sick children, not having it in his power to relieve their sufferings.

In the morning he resolvd to procure water for the dying children. He made his way to the bank of the stream, where he was discoverd by an Indian and shot at. He fell as if dead, remaind a short time and then secreted himself in the brush. While lying on the bank, a friendly Indian made known the fact to his wife, but advisd her not to go to him as it would discover him to the murderers. How intense must have been her feelings.

About sundown Mr. Kimble left his retreat with the apparent intention of going in to his family. He reachd the corner of the garden fence some five rods from his door, where he was shot by Frank Askaloom, who afterwards took his daughter, the amiable Miss Kimble, for a wife. He claimd her as a right for having killd her father, of which he would often speak, to her with the air and appearance of one who had done her an invaluable favor.

Who can attempt to measure the deep horror and anguish of soul, of a young woman in such hands! May kind Heaven prevent a like affliction to any of his sinful children. Her bitter weeping whenever the Indian spoke of killing her father had the effect only to induce him to propose to exchange her to another Indian who held another of the captive young women as a wife.

Why Mr. Kimble did not attempt to make his escape on Monday night, or why, after having livd out the day on Tuesday, he did not remain in his retreat till dark and then escape, is not known. He was heard to say on Monday night, "It matters but little when we die if we are but prepard." Perhaps the pain of his arm took away the strength of resolution. Perhaps he chose rather to die in the bosom of his family, than to make the uncertain attempt to save his life, which could only be a living death while wife and children remaind captives in the hands of the murderers, the sport of their beastly passions, the victims of their cruelty. For a stranger to reach my place one hundred and twenty miles, traveling nights, there was no reasonable hope, and if he could, he might end the nights of travel and pain and days of watching and hunger only to mingle his own with the dead bodies of the slain of that station—for what mind could divine where the work of superstition would end, which had no power to fear, and many inducements to go forward?

The Dalls were equally hopeless for like reasons.

Fort Walla-walla could afford a safe retreat, but unfortunately it was in the hands of Papists, for whom Mr. K. had the strongest fears as he expresd himself to me the week before his death—for no other reason can we account for his not fleeing to that fort Monday night. Had he done so, it is not probable the fate of poor Mr. Hall would have stood alone upon the page of history, to teach our children that Romanism is in practice what it is in theory, UNCHANGEABLE.

No horse arriving, Mr. Camfield left his hiding-place, and wound his way up the narrow skirt of brush till he came to what he supposd to be the trail to my place, about dark. In a country cut up with trails, Providence directed his feet to the right one, which he pursued that night and the next day, when Wednesday night found him in the deep valley of the Taka-nan, where he slept.

Thursday he followd the fresh tracks of cattle, which brought him at night to the brink of Snake River bluffs, some miles below the regular route.

Friday morning he came to the river, and having no fear from the Nez Perces, he calld to their camp on the opposite side and was crossd over. The Indian driving the cattle conducted Mr. C. to my house upon one of his horses, for which he requird his buffalo robe. That night they staid in a camp on the Clear Water, nine miles below my house.

Intelligence of the massacre had not yet reachd the Nez Perces, and Mr. C. was careful to avoid any intimation. Had it been known in any of these camps, he would have been killd.

Saturday late in the afternoon, Mr. C. reachd my house and communicated to Mrs. Spalding the horrible intelligence of the massacre, aggravated by the probability that the body of her husband had been added to the slain, as he supposd, from the report of the guns on Tuesday. If not slain at that time, there was no human probability that I could escape. Five days had already elapsd and I had not arrivd, which made it quite certain that I had been killd.

The case, of itself sufficient to overwhelm the stoutest soul, was greatly aggravated by the fact, that her daughter was a captive in the hands of the murderers of her husband, who would proceed immediately to that defenseless station, to add her brother and the other Americans at the station, to the number of the dead, and herself and remaining children, to the already long catalogue of living victims of the savage cruelties.

There was scarcely the shadow of protection in the few Americans at the place, and she was too well acquainted with the close relationship existing between the Cayuse and Nez Perces, and the treachery of the Indian character, to place any confidence in the Indians of the place, except motives of self-interest should appear.

But she was entirely in their hands. There was no other alternative, and with the self possession and calmness of mind peculiarly her own, in moments of imminent peril, she resolvd to make known the awful fact, and cast herself and children into the hands of the principal men of the place. Mr. Camfield begd of her not to do so, but evidently it was the salvation of all at the station. Had the people of the place remaind ignorant of the awful deed, till the report was brought by Indians—doubtless the bloody scenes of the Waiilatpu would have been repeated at Clear Water. The first Indian arrivd with the intelligence of the massacre, on Monday, a Nez Perces,—doubtless a participator in the bloody crime. But he was accompanied by a band of Nez Perces from the camp, at which Mr. Camfield staid Friday night, with the avowd purpose of plundering the station of all the property, which, of course,—would have ended in killing the men, and perhaps Mrs. Spalding, and captivating Miss Johnson and the children. They were prevented by the chiefs, and their people of the place, to whom Mrs. S. had committed herself.

On the arrival of Mr. Camfield, Mr. Hart, the brother of Mrs. S. was not at the house. Providentially Jacob and Shakantai, (Eagle,) two principal chiefs, were at the house, to whom Mrs. S. communicated the astounding intelligence. While one communicated the news to the camp, the other carrid a hasty note to Mr. Craig, living ten miles up the branch. The Indians immediately flew to the protection of Mr. S. and the house.

Among those who showd themselves friendly were Luke and his two brothers, members of our church, Jacob, about to be receivd into the church,

James, a Catholic, but particularly friendly to myself and family, and most of their people. Some of old James' people, united with the robbers, and took considerable property.

The Indians decided that Mrs. S. with her effects, must be removd to Mr. Craig's, where they were taking up their winter quarters, on account of wood. They judgd that the Cayuse would be there without delay, and they could not protect the family, so far from their camp. Mrs. S. proposd to remain quiet over the Sabbath. James and one or two others remaind as a guard. The rest retird. Mr. Craig came down late at night. Mrs. S. endeavord to start an express to Tishimakair, the station of bros. Walker and Eells, but no Indian could be inducd to go. She next besought the Indians to send an express for her daughter, if found alive, and to learn the fate of her husband.—They objected, alleging that the women and children were without doubt all killd. She finally told them she was jealous of every one of them, and could not feel that she had a friend among them. It had the desird effect. The Eagle consented to undertake it, still others threw difficulties in his way, and it was near night the next day, before he started.

Mr. Camfield's wound was much inflamd, by wading the streams, and traveling. He receivd a shot in his side from a pistol, the ball still remaining in the flesh.

Mr. Jackson, it will be recollected, accompanied me to Waiilatpu, and was waiting my return from the Utilla, till Monday forenoon, when a slight circumstance inducd him to leave for Clear Water, about three hours before the massacre commencd. He reachd Mr. Craig's Tuesday night, ignorant of what had taken place, and of his own narrow escape.

There was another band of Indians encampd in the same valley, some ten miles from my station, headed by Joseph,—a principal chief, in the absence of Ellis.

Joseph was one of the first natives who gave evidence of a change of heart, and united with the church 8 years ago, and had, up to this time, with the exception of two or three slight deviations, exhibited a good Christian character.

Many of Joseph's people were campd with him, and cultivated extensively in the valley, and had for the last four or five years, constituted a good portion of the Sabbath congregation—and the school. Seven of them were members of the church, and had ever appeard friendly to the mission.

Their present movements however, were very suspicious.—Almost daily, Joseph with many of his people, had been in the habit of visiting the house. But after the arrival of the news of the massacre, neither Joseph nor any of his people showd themselves till Monday morning, when many of the latter, and among them, Joseph's brother-in-law, and from the same fire—showd themselves with the robbers, and were foremost in plundering the buildings.

Here was an opportunity for religion to show itself, if there was any. Never before had temptation come to Joseph and his native brethren, in the ch. in this dress. But now it came, and his fall, as I regard it, and that of some others, has given to the Christian world a lesson that should be well studied, before it again places the lives and property of missionaries at the mercy of lawless savages, without a military force to keep them in awe.

THINGS IN OREGON

CHAPTER XVI

Arrival of Gov. Lane—Description of Port Astoria and vicinity—Narrow escape from Shipwreck.

March 8th, 1849.—I am quietly stowd away in a private family in Oregon city, after having roamd up and down the valley, in pursuit of information.

All is commotion here. Gov. Lane, from Indiana, arrivd in town the first of this month, bringing the new government with him in his pocket up the Willamet river in a skiff, over the Clackamas rapids. As to whether he got out and helpd to pull the boat over the rapids or not, I have not been informd. The big men of the place are brushing up their boots and putting on their best clothes, as the Governor passes the streets, hoping as he passes along, that his eye may fall upon them placidly. I do not very well know what such things mean, though I suppose that politicians do.

April 7th.—The first public mail arrivd in Oregon city, from the U. States, by the mail steamer of San Francisco, to-day. This country begins to be alive to maritime business—the first vessel ever built at the Willamet falls in Oregon, is now on the stocks. Her owners say her tunnage will be from 50 to 60 tuns burden.

After having staid in Oregon nearly seven months, I take my departure from Oregon city, the 10th of April, for San Francisco, by way of the ocean.

Port Astoria, *26th.*—To-day embarkd on board ship for San Francisco bay, after having staid nearly two weeks at Astoria, waiting for the ship to be in readiness to leave. My stay at this place has given me an opportunity of learning something of this part of the country, the difficulty of navigating the river at this part of it, and the prices of some articles of produce, as sold here in these times of great excitement.

Port Astoria is situated about 15 miles from the mouth of the Columbia river, on the south side of it. The place has not been improvd since its first establishment. There are only five or six houses in the place that have been built by the whites, excepting a storehouse or two built by the Hudson Bay

Company. The country here and around Astoria, is rugged and unpleasant, heavily coverd with fir and hemlock, some of which is of giant size.

About 25 miles of the river from its mouth, is indented with bays by various names, making a width of from 7 to 10 or 12 miles.

At the mouth of the river, on the north, is Cape Disappointment.

Eight miles distant, on the opposite side, is Clatsap point, sometimes calld Point Adams.

Cape Disappointment, by its projection from the main land, forms a little cove, calld Baker's bay. Here ships may lie in perfect safety.

On the south side, higher up, at the entrance of Young into the Lewis and Clark's river, is Young's bay.

At the mouth of the Columbia river, between Cape Disappointment and Clatsap point, is an extensive sand-bar, which renders an entrance to the river difficult, except by experiencd navigators of the river.

The first 15 or 20 miles of the entrance of the river, has a channel so crooked that almost every point of compass is traversd, which makes navigation by sail ships slow and dangerous. At every new point, ships are obligd oftentimes to stop several days and sometimes weeks for a change of wind. The only successful and speedy mode of traversing the river will ultimately be by steam vessels.

Amongst other things that have fallen within my notice whilst at Astoria, was the price of a few articles of produce brought to this place to sell to passengers, whilst waiting for the readiness of the ship. Potatoes were sold at one dollar per bushel, eggs at $1 per dozen, butter at $1 per pound. Flour a little more moderate—its price per barrel was only $10. During my stay at Astoria, a beef was killd at Clatsap and brought here, and sold at 12 cents for the fore, and 15 for the hind quarters, per pound.

27th.—On leaving Astoria, our ship was thrown on the beach, where she remaind during the day, occasiond by the drunkenness of our pilot.

Thursday, May 3d, we left Baker's bay for the broad ocean, with a fair wind and high hopes of crossing the sand-bar with pleasantness and safety. The number of souls on board was about 130. We proceeded gently along for three-fourths of an hour, when we arrivd near the place where the ships Shark, Vancouver and Maine were wreckd, and the wind nearly ceasd to blow. Our ship became unmanageable, drifting by the strong tide which was then unfavorable, and likely in a few minutes to carry us from the channel and place us upon the sands, where the ship must inevitably have become a wreck.

In this critical situation, with only 18 feet of water for a ship drawing 15, and the tide yet falling—by the energetic movement of our officers and crew, they were enabld to stay the ship by immediately casting anchor. After waiting more than 2 hours in this perilous situation, the wind became of sufficient strength to justify an attempt to make our escape by parting anchor.

During this time of extreme anxiety, soundings were constantly kept up both on ship and at a distance around.

When all things were ready on board for the attempt, orders were given and instantly the anchor with 180 feet of chain were severd from the ship, and she under way in a retrograde course towards Cape Disappointment. We continud our retrograde course till we arrivd as near the cape as practicable, in consequence of a bar which projected a short distance from it, at which point we changd our course to the south-west, and in less than one hour we were in the broad ocean, and over all danger from sand-bars.

Monday evening, 9 o'clock, May 7th.—Safely anchord in San Francisco bay. Our passage from the time we were relievd at the Columbia bar, may be reckond at 96 hours' sailing. More than 12 of this was under extremely moderate wind, though in a favorable direction. The remainder of the way, was under a very strong breeze. It would seem then, that the distance may be saild, with a strong wind, in about 3½ days, which is about 560 miles, by the way of the ocean.

To my great astonishment, on looking about on the morning of the 8th, I counted about 60 vessels of various sizes lying in the bay, most of which were inactive for want of men to work them, they having left for the mines. On passing up the St. Waukeen, the course of my first visit to the mines, I saw scatterd along at different points, many more vessels of various sizes.

The present head of navigation for sail ships, is a little cloth town calld Stocton. Here were 8 or 10 more vessels lying disrobd of their sails to make cloth houses of. This town is more than 100 miles up from San Francisco. At this place, supplies are deposited for the mines, which are carrid by wagons and pack animals, to the mining district, a distance of 70 or 80 miles further, upon the tributaries of the Saint Waukeen.

GOLD MANIA, OR YELLOW FEVER, AS SOME CALL IT

CHAPTER XVII

Excitement in Oregon, relative to the discovery of Gold in California.

The discovery of the Gold District in California, has producd the greatest excitement of any thing of a similar nature in modern days.

The first commencement of the excitement in Oregon was about the middle of August, 1848, and within one month's time, nearly 2000 persons left Oregon for that place.

The district is said to be the richest ever known. Though it is questionable whether the gold obtaind by Solomon was not found equally abundant, since among so great a number of citizens as Jerusalem furnishd, the abundance of gold in that place had reducd the value of silver to almost nothing.

When the news of gold in California reachd Oregon, the wheat harvest was not yet ended, and so great was the delirium when the news arrivd, that many of the farmers left their fields unfinishd, giving them up gratuitously to any one who might be disposd to harvest them, or let them waste upon the ground.

As late as the 10th of March, 1849, the fever continud with unabated fury, increasing in its sanguinary features as the warm season approachd, preying upon the heart and vitals of every human being in Oregon.

From the 13th of Sept. last, which was the time I arrivd at Oregon city, to the 10th of March following, not one day passd, Sundays not excepted, without the mention by some one in my presence, of the gold speculation.

During the remainder of my stay in Oregon city, tools of various kinds were invented and being made at that place, ready for departure to the mines, so soon as they might be profitably worked, on the opening of the warm season.

The following description of the Gold Mania is taken from the Oregon Spectator, as quoted from the Californian—

GOLD MINES OF CALIFORNIA

In our paper of August 16, we devoted considerable space to the subject of the gold mines, stating some facts in regard to their discovery, and the manner in which the ore was collected. So well was the article receivd by the public—then on the *qui vive* for information about the mines—and consequently so great the demand for our paper, that in a few hours after publication the entire edition was disposd of. Since then we have receivd many and urgent demands for that number of the Californian, and this week, at the solicitation of a number of our patrons, we repeat the substance of our former article, with some additional particulars.

It appears that in the first part of February last, Messrs. Marshall and Bennett were engagd with a party in erecting a saw-mill for Capt. J. A. Sutter, on the American fork of the Sacramento river, about 40 miles above its mouth. In excavating the tail-race, they removd the rock during the day, and let in the water during the night, in order to wash out the loose dirt and sand. On the morning of the 10th, after shutting off the water, Mr. Marshall discoverd the first gold, lying upon decomposd granite, in the bottom of the race.

It would seem that but little doubt was entertaind of its being the real *simon pure*, for operations immediately ceasd on the mill, and all hands commencd searching for gold. It was soon found that gold abounded along the American fork for a distance of 30 miles. For a time the discoverers were the only ones aware of the fact, but the news finally spread through the settlements. But little credit however was gaind by the report, though occasionally a solitary "gold hunter" might be seen stealing down to a launch with a pick and shovel, more than half ashamd of his credulity.

Some time during the month of May, a number of credible persons arrivd in town from the scene of operations, bringing specimens of the ore, and stating that those engagd in collecting the precious metal were making from $3 to $10 per day.

Then commencd the grand rush!

The inhabitants throughout the territory were in commotion. Large companies of men, women and children could be seen on every road leading to the mines, their wagons loaded down with tools for digging, provisions, &c. Launch after launch left the wharves of our city, crowded with passengers and freight for the Sacramento.

Mechanical operations of every kind ceasd—whole streets, that were but a week before alive with a busy population, were entirely deserted, and the place wore the appearance of a city that had been suddenly visited by a devastating plague. To cap the climax, newspapers were obligd to stop printing for want of readers.

Meantime our mercantile friends were doing an unusual "stroke" of business. Every arrival from the mining district brought more or less gold dust, the major part of which immediately passd into the hands of the merchants for goods, &c. Immense quantities of merchandize were conveyd to the mines, until it became a matter of astonishment where so much could be disposd of. During the first eight weeks of the "golden times" the receipts at this place in gold dust amounted to $250,000. For the eight weeks ending at this date, they were $600,000.

The number of persons now engagd in gold hunting, will probably exceed 6000, including Indians, and one ounce per day, is the lowest average we can put for each person, while many collect their hundreds of dollars, for a number of days in succession, and instances have been known where one individual has collected from $1500, to $1800 worth of pure gold in a day.

Explorations have been progressing, and it is now fully ascertaind that gold exists on both sides of the Sierra Nevada from lat. 41 North, to as far South, as the head waters of the San Joaquin river, a distance of 400 miles in length, and 100 in breadth. Farther than this has not been explord, but from the nature of the country beyond the sources of the San Joaquin, we doubt not gold will also be found there in equal abundance. The gold region already known, is however sufficiently extensive to give profitable employment to 100,000 persons for generations to come. The ore is in a virgin state, disseminated in small doses, and is found in three distinct deposits,—sand and graveld beds, on decomposd granite, and intermixd with a kind of slate.

For a long time subsequent to the discovery of the mines,—the only implements usd in washing the gold, were large tin pans, or Indian baskets. Latterly, 'machines were usd—at first, a rough log hollowd out (in some, instances,) by burning and scraping with a butcher knife—afterwards, more finishd ones made their appearance, built of red wood boards, in the shape of an ordinary trough, about ten feet long, and two feet wide at the top, with a riddle or sive at one end to catch the larger gravel, and three or four small bars at the bottom, about ½ an inch high, to keep the gold from going out with the dirt and water at the lower end. This machine is set upon rockers,— which gives a half rotary motion to the dirt and water inside.'—Four men are requisite to work one of these machines properly.

Within the past month, many sick persons from the mines have arrivd at this place, and scarcely a launch comes down the Sacramento, without more or less sick persons on board,—while some die on the river. The very natural inference drawn from this, by those who have never been at the mines, is, that they lie in a sickly section of the country, and those at work there, are in daily expectation of being sick. In our opinion,—however, nothing can be farther from the truth. As far as our experience goes, it is on the large rivers only, where disease prevails, and in passing up and down upon them, the person not in perfect health is almost invariably the one to become sick.—We have observd but few, very few cases of sickness in the immediate neighborhood of the mines, but such as we believe would have occurd under similar circumstances in any other climate. Let the miner pass the Sacramento safely, (and we would almost insure any person's doing so that was perfectly regular and temperate in all his habits,)—let him not, when he arrives at the mines, work as though he was privilegd to operate for a limited time only, but poco poco, resting at proper intervals,—let him abstain from the free use of intoxicating drinks, living upon wholesome food,—avoiding, for instance, half baked bread—let him sleep under the shelter of a tent, with warm bedding,—and if, after following our advice in all these particulars, the gold hunter becomes sick, why—we do not know anything about the matter.

CALIFORNIA GOLD MINES DESCRIBED

CHAPTER XVIII

Geography of the Gold District of Alta California.

From recent searches for gold in Northern California, it appears that the present gold district is comprisd, nearly all of it, within the following boundary. It lies on the western declivity of the Sierra Neveda range of mountains, and gold is sought for along the tributaries of the great Sacramento river in the northern, and the St. Waukeen river in the southern part of Northern or Upper California.

The names of the tributaries of the St. Waukeen, beginning with the most northern one, are as follows. Makelemas, which unites with the Saint Waukeen, near its confluence with the Sacramento. Next south, is Calaveras. South of this, is Stanislaus. The next important river, is Twalamy. Still farther south, a distance of 20 or 25 miles, is a considerable stream, calld Merced, or River of Mercy. South of Merced, is another, calld Mereposa, though I believe this is dry part of the year. These constitute the principal mountain streams, tributary to the St. Waukeen.

The names of the rivers in the northern mining district, tributaries to the Sacramento, are, first and nearest the confluence of the Sacramento with the St. Waukeen, the Cosumnes. Next northward, the American river, the largest tributary to the Sacramento. It has several forks, calld North, South and Middle forks of the American river. Next, Rio de los Plumos or Feather river. Still farther north, are Bear, Quesnels and Sycamore rivers.

The length from north to south, of the present gold district, cannot well be computed at more than 400 miles, lying within the latitudes of 36 and 42 deg. north. In its width, which is mostly contain within a distance of from 20 to 30 miles, it traverses the middle portion of the western declivity of the aforementiond range of mountains, though miners assert that gold has been found sparingly, high up some of the mountain streams, toward its axis.

The whole surface of the gold district presents one continud scene of uneven country. Much of it, the hills soar far above the intervening valleys below—and along some of the principal tributaries, for miles in length, very deep kanions are formd.

The water of the large streams is very pure and healthy, being mostly from the melted snows of the mountain. During the summer season it seldom rains, and the rivers continue to fall, till quite along into the winter season. After the rainy season commences, which is most powerful toward the summit of the mountains, floods are often witnessd low down the streams, where not a single drop of water has fallen for months. These floods descend with a mighty rush, and often surprise the miner before he is able to remove his mining implements from the bed of a stream.

The mining district is coverd with a thin growth of scrub oaks and yellow pine. The earth is divested of soil, except sparingly in some of the valleys, being of a reddish color, by the decomposition of rocks containing iron.

The climate is so dry during summer, that little grass grows in any part of the mines. Nauseous exhalations are therefore excluded, and the atmosphere is quite healthy. In some parts of the mines the miners become sick, but it is mostly attributable to their treatment with themselves. Through the summer months, the days are warm but the nights are cool, and but few nights occur in which a man does not need considerable night clothing toward morning.

CHAPTER XIX

The Geology of the Gold District of California, with the
probable cause of the production of Gold to the surface of
the earth.

The rocks of Golden California, in common with the whole western declivity of the Sierra Neveda mountains, are principally composd of primary, stratified, slate rocks. Some of these rocks are talcose slate. Others are more silicious, approaching even to coarsish sandstone slate, of various colors.

Before confining the reader expressly to the gold district, a few remarks relative to that portion of California lying west of the Neveda mountains to the valley of the great Sacramento and St. Waukeen, may afford some light on the subject of that part of the western declivity lying within the seat of mining operations. The slate rock on the western side of the mountain range, from its axis to its base, is tilted up a little more than perpendicularly outward from the axis of the mountain, a distance of more than 60 miles in width, and traverses the whole range, as far north and south as the present mines extend, in lines parallel to the course of the mountain's axis.

At the base of the mountain, commences a tertiary deposit of about 20 miles in width, which, with an alluvial deposit of about 20 more in width, to the great rivers of the valley, hides from sight the remaining portion of tilted rocks, so that the entire width of the tilted strata can never exactly be ascertaind. But if a mountain range like the one under consideration, is formd by the furrowd and ridgd condition of the earth's crust, by conforming to a diminishd molten nucleus within, from refrigeration of its heat, it may be expected that the whole declivity, from its axis or highest point to its lowest or mid valley, may be all of it tilted up in the same manner as that portion which is presented to sight. If this be fact, we are then apprizd that a portion of the earth's crust must have had a thickness of full 100 miles, by measuring across the tilted rocks, from the central valley, to the top of the mountain, eastward,—a fact not hitherto believd by geologists, from experiments made upon the increase of downward heat, to where the crust must necessarily become molten.

As so many and various opinions of the tilted condition of primary stratified rocks have been advancd among the visitants of the gold district of California, a few conflicting opinions may serve in some degree to satisfy the mind of the curious.

It is the belief of some, that rocks cannot have become tilted without the expansive powr of volcanic agency. Hence, on viewing the country around, they imagine they see successions of craters, formd all over the western declivity of the Neveda mountains, and in some places, profusions of scoria bestrewing the ground. For my own part, I must confess that I have seen nothing in my ramblings to justify a belief that volcanic agency any where has existed so as to produce the present appearance of those rocks.

Those persons imagining volcanic agency in those parts, are not aware that intense heat destroys stratification, for in the middle of the craters of some of their imaginary volcanoes, the stratification is as perfect as in any other portion of the tilted district, and they are not apprizd that in such case a discrepancy must therefore exist.

After the tilting of those rocks had occurd, it would not be improbable, with such an enormous crust resting entirely upon a liquid, molten nucleus, that many undulations in it should occur, and in many instances the crust should become weakend and even sunderd apart by the severe strain. Into fissures so formd, granite, sandstone and conglomerated rocks, may have subsequently been intruded, presenting, therefore, to persons unacquainted with such rocks, the appearances of craters, scoria, &c. In some parts of New England, primary stratified rocks are tilted up confusedly, having no regular line of strike. In some cases, the dynamics employd may have been volcanic, or they may have been paroxysmal, acting from time to time, till those rocks were thrown into their present condition. But tilted rocks that have a regular line of strike, must have a regular agency to place them in such condition. Hence, then, considering the perfect parallelism of the tilted rocks of Golden California with the mountain axis, it seems to follow, that an exceedingly slow and regular movement of the tilting of those rocks must have occurd.

Another consideration of the western declivity of the Neveda mountains, is in relation to the formation of its rivers.

Almost invariably, the rivers of Oregon were formd by an expansive force from beneath, but the rivers of California were formd by undulations in the earth's crust, which is well proven by the entire passage of unbroken strata across the beds of streams. Such condition of its rocks, is also another proof against volcanic agency in those parts.

The inquiring mind may now be led to the subject of Quartz Rock, containd among the slate rock of the gold district.

The quartz rock of the gold region is mostly white, though some of it is of the carnelian order, whilst some is translucent, and other specimens are entirely transparent. The carnelian appearance of some of the quartz seems to have been nothing more than the circulation of water containing the red oxide of iron, through the cracks of the broken quartz, till the rock became tingd with it. The transparent variety is crystalizd, and is found only sparingly.

Quartz is found interstratified amongst the tilted slate, varying from less than one quarter of an inch in thickness to several feet, and in some places even to rods, penetrating the slate indefinitely downward.

Although quartz is mostly seen lying in a position parallel with the stratified slate rock, yet in some instances it is found crossing it diagonally.

To account for the formation of quartz and its occupying its present position in the gold district, is to account also for the formation and production of gold to the surface of the earth, as is satisfactorily believd by all. It is hard to account for much of the works of nature. If it be considerd, that the quartz veins of the gold district be of aqueous origin, that is, formd by infiltration, or the percolation of silicious water into unoccupied spaces, till they are completely filld with silicious sediment, so as to become rock, we then have to account for its existing there in a friable state, which is hard to conceive, since a formation by aqueous agency would most likely produce solid rock.

It is equally hard to see how gold can be found imbedded in solid masses in those quartz veins, since, if by the percolation of the water, quartz was producd there, so also must the gold have been producd by infiltration—and in such case, it must have been disseminated through the whole rock, giving hues of various shades, as is the case with iron in a soluble state.

Another objection to the formation of the quartz of the gold district by infiltration, is, that it is not generally transparent, since the percolation of silicious water through cold and silent places will most naturally produce such result. It is most probable that the crystalizd portion of those rocks was formd from silicious water, after the original deposit.

It has been asserted by some miners, that they have seen gold in a state of formation, by the percolation of water over quartz rock. Those men are probably such as believe that quartz is the mother of gold—and by the way, I should like to have them tell me also what the father was. They say that the yellow appearance of the mud and other sedimentary matter, which they have seen passing through quartz veins, is gold in a state of formation. Perhaps they might allow of a correction in their minds on that subject, if they were told that the yellow appearance they saw was nothing more than decomposd iron—probably the chromate of it.

Another view of the subject may be taken, somewhat like the following. It may be considerd that the quartz of the gold district was formd previous to the tilting up of the slate rock, by alternations of tabular masses with the slate.

Some objections to this mode also naturally arise. One objection is, that there are instances of quartz veins traversing the stratified slate rock diagonally. Another is, that it cannot well be conceivd that so thin layers, as is the case with some of the quartz rock, can well be formd in a tabular way. And if the quartz had been formd by alternate layers with the stratified slate, it must of necessity have been of aqueous origin, and also the gold.

The last view I shall take of the quartz, as found interstratified with the slate rock, is, that the slate rock is of aqueous origin, and the quartz rock of igneous origin, intruded from beneath after the tilting up of the slate.

In the formation of stratified rocks, the planes of stratification, or sides facing each other, are never firmly united together, being formd by depositions from water at different times, so that by subsequent movements they are liable to be sunderd apart. If it now be considerd the enormity of a massive crust of earth resting upon a molten nucleus, it becomes easy to see how intrusions upward of melted matter can take place amongst stratified rocks, and the many undulatory movements of the rocks, as appear in the mining district, only give facility to its accomplishment.

If it be taken for fact, that the quartz of the mining district was intruded in a melted state, it must also be considerd that gold was intruded with it. To account for the friable state of the quartz, moisture must be suppos'd to have been present, whilst the quartz was in a heated state.

Such a state of things would produce a disintegration of the quartz rock, and set at liberty the imbedded gold, to be carrid downward by gravitation from the hills into ravines, creeks and rivers. To account next, for the difference between massive imbedded gold in quartz rock, and gold disseminated in small particles, needs only to consider the quartz acting as a flux during a state of fusion, to bring the gold together, in the same manner as borax, glass or quartz will do in the artist's crucible—and the only probable difference between the gold of California and that of Georgia, is, during a melted state of the quartz, a higher degree of heat existed in the quartz of California than that of Georgia, thereby bringing about a more perfect work of separation between the quartz and the gold.

CHAPTER XX

Three varieties of Gold, with their distinctions, and the reasons given why they are found in separate localities.—Philosophy of running water.

FIRST VARIETY

The first variety of Gold may be considerd as that which is in dry ravines, or between hills, where there is no running water, except in the time of showers, or the melting of snows.—This variety is calld dry ravine or angular gold, from the fact that whatever be its form, whether in plates or heavy solid masses, or in thin scales,—the edges are all sharp and angular, as nature formd it, having never been rounded off by attrition among moving pebbles or sand, in violent streams of water. The agent of deposit seems to have been mostly that of gravitation during the decomposition of the rocks of the hills containing gold, aided probably by the moistening influences of rains upon the alluvium of the hills, and the general movement of alluvium from higher to lower levels. When once deposited in these situations, it never after receives a secondary removal, except by the hand of the miner.

Dry ravine deposits vary in their advantages for obtaining gold, according to the slope of the hills, through which the ravine passes. At the heads of ravines, where the country is but an undulating one, of moderate hills, and wide-spread valleys, the deposits are generally so disseminated, that but little advantages are gaind, by searching for gold in such situations.

Downward, towards the mouths of ravines, where the hills are in close contiguity, gold is deposited in a line along the center of ravines, varying somewhat in richness, according to the richness of the adjoining hills that deposited it, or the inclination, or basin-shapd appearance of the ravine along its course to its mouth. If ravines are of rapid descent from their sources to their outlets, they mostly contribute their gold to the streams into which they empty themselves.

SECOND VARIETY

The second variety of gold is that which is creek-washd,—the corners and edges of which are rounded off by attrition among moving pebbles and sand of the tertiary deposits of creeks, during the time of freshets. This gold, whether found in plates, or rounded masses, is most of it too heavy to float in running water, being carrid onward to its place of rest, by the united agency of gravitation, moving water, and the tertiary sediment.

The creeks and large rivers receive their gold from the mouths of ravines and hills contiguous to the creeks and rivers.

Gold is found in dry ravines, creeks, and in basins of rivers, weighing several ounces.

In some places along the creeks, the miner finds angular gold deposited in the banks of the streams at the foot of a hill, where it had not slidden down sufficiently far to reach the power of the waters of the stream.

Lost, or erratic gold is sometimes found in the creeks among the creek-washd sand and gravel of the stream, being subject to occasional removals, by subsequent freshets. Such gold seems to be on its way to its final deposit or resting place in situations where subsequent freshets can take no effect upon it for further removal.

Some of this gold is in pieces of several dollars value, but most of it is in fine grains, with a mixture of floating gold.

The fine gold is found in situations above the rock, in deposits of loose sand, where every violent freshet gives it another removal, till it is ultimately carrid downward and deposited in the bars of the large rivers.

THIRD VARIETY

The third variety of gold is that which may be denominated bar, scale, or floating gold. This gold is found in the tertiary deposits, commonly calld bars of the large streams flowing down from the Neveda range of mountains. Hence the name of bar gold.

Its form is that of very thin scales, which causes it to float in waters that are highly agitated. Hence also, the names of scale, and floating gold.

This gold is seldom found in pieces worth more than a dollar, and is rounded off by attrition, the same as the creek-washd gold.

The several varieties here describd, were the same, only differing in form, in the original rock—but the several agents of deposit, have separated them into separate classes, according to the several capacities of gold to receive the power of the several depositing agents. Hence, the finest floating gold is found lowest down the principal rivers, where it is deposited. Creek-washd gold, being heavy, is never movd very far down the stream, from where it was first deposited into it—and dry ravine gold, having still a little different agent from the others, has never been movd but a very short distance.

If no more could be said of water, than of other matter of the earth, that it seeks rest by gravitation, in common with the harder portions of matter, but little of its influences could ever be known, to what is now apparent, when viewd in all its bearings. But the fluidity of water, gives it advantages over other matter, in possessing movements, which the latter can never receive—such as lateral motion, capillary attraction, great expansion by heat, aerial passages from rare to dense mediums, thereby giving a new preparation to descend in the form of rain or snow, to restore again its former equilibrium.

Running water, in the light here intended to be explaind, is that which flows down rivers and creeks, from higher to lower levels. Water, like all other substances, will fall perpendicularly from higher to lower levels, if there be no interposing obstacle. But as the beds of streams descend like an inclind plane, from their sources to their mouths, water is forcd over them by the power of gravitation, till it arrives at a level with other surrounding water, and is thereby prevented from descending further. Now in the movement of water, along its downward passage, many considerations arise.

First, if water were made to pass downward thro' a straight duct or channel, whose lateral and vertical sides were perfectly smooth, so that no friction could exist between the water and the trough or duct that containd it, there would be no eddy formd along its sides, for the water would all of it have a straight forward, and downward movement.

But as the bottom and edges of streams are rough and uneven, very frequent obstructions to water occur. Places so obstructed, are the eddies or partial eddies, so commonly observable in streams of running water.

If an observer stands on the bank of a creek, during a time of high water, where there is much irregularity and unevenness of its bottom, he will see in some places, that the water is nearly motionless—in others, a whirling round of the water,—in others, a retrograde or up stream motion. Under all the circumstances of these several appearances of the water, those places that are the most quiet, approach nearest to the most perfect eddies.

Wherever a bend in a creek occurs, the water, by an opposing bank, is forcd to take a new direction, passing downward, along on its inclind, though uneven bottom. The opposing bank stops a portion of the flowing waters, and causes them to turn back, along the shore of the creek, producing, thereby,—a section of inactive waters, between those of the downward and those of the upward course.

Again, if a lateral stream of water flows into a creek, similar or nearly so in magnitude, the two partially opposing currents form an eddy in the upper angle of the two, and an eddy of less magnitude, is also formd in the angle of the two, on the lower side of the lateral stream.

When water passes over a reef of rock, that traverses entirely across the stream, like a mill dam, the central waters or current cannot well form an eddy immediately below the reef, on account of its impetuous movement — though laterally, towards the banks, partial quietness of the water may exist.

If an obstacle, as a rock or other body, protrude in the current of a creek, so high that water is forcd around it, instead of running over it, an eddy is formd immediately below it, in magnitude according to the size of the obstacle.

CHAPTER XXI

Mode of searching for Gold in California.

Rock gold, or that which is disseminated in dust or fine particles amongst quartz rock, being so rare in California, but little attention is paid to searching for it in such situations.

Mode of Searching for the First Variety

The miner, in prospecting for the first variety, or dry ravine gold, selects a situation where, judging from the appearance of the hills, or the slope of the ravine likely to contain gold, it may be found most abundant. He commences his excavation at the center of the ravine, by digging downward till he arrives in most cases at the rock on which the deposit was made, which varies from 2 to 10 or 15 feet in depth. He then prospects outward toward the hills till he arrives at the line of deposit, in case any deposit there exists.

After having found a lead of gold, he excavates upward and downward the ravine, being careful whilst progressing along, to watch the several meanderings of the lead, which are likely to occur even in very short distances.

The miner never need be long at a loss to determine whether there be gold in the place where he is prospecting. If gold exists only in moderate quantities, the pick will generally detect it by occasionally throwing out into view pieces of gold, even when they are quite small. In digging in dry ravines, the miner, after having arrivd within a few inches of the rock where he expects to find gold, tries the earth by washing some of it. If he finds no gold, all of the earth above this place is thrown away as useless. He then continues to dig downward, trying the dirt at short intervals, till he finds gold in his washings. He then is careful to save and wash all of the remainder that lies above the rock, and even to pick off a few inches from the top of some rocks that are loose and open enough to receive gold in some of their crevices, carefully saving and washing the whole.

In some instances in dry ravines, where slate rock occurs, it is decomposd into clay, to a considerable depth, from the vast amount of time elapsd since it has been placd in its present situation. Where such decomposition has occurd, it is useless to penetrate downward into it, in search of gold, as the gold was deposited most generally in a strong iron deposit, previous to the decomposition of the rock. This strong iron deposit is formd of soluble iron, amongst which the gold is mechanically entangld and there held, unless the iron becomes again soluble and leaves the gold to settle down by gravitation into the decomposd rock below. Cases of the second solubility of the iron do not often occur in dry ravines.

Mode of Searching for the Second Variety

It is more difficult to point out a successful mode of searching for gold of the second variety than either of the other two. Yet notwithstanding the difficulties attending it, some hints may be given, useful to the miner, who has previously become in some degree acquainted with the philosophy of running water and the nature of tertiary deposits.

Those creeks of intermediate size between dry ravines, and the large rivers flowing down from the mountains, though dry or nearly so at some seasons of the year, are powrful in times of heavy rains or the rapid melting of snows, as is evident from the position of some heavy rocks in those streams, which none other agent the powr of a mighty stream could have placd there.

In prospecting for gold in those creeks, the miner may select a position which he judges to be the channel of the creek, or that portion of it where the greatest powr of water is exerted, and commence digging downward, till he arrives at the rock over which various tertiary sediment has flowd, and if he finds the coarse gravel and sand through which he passes, entirely down to the rock, cleanly washd of alluvium, he may fairly conclude that he is in the current of that stream, or where the water passes with greatest force. In those situations, he rarely finds gold, or if he does, it is in sparing quantities.

If upon arriving at the rock, he finds a cross reef or ledge rock, rising one foot or more above the rocks downward stream from his position, he may then prospect outward either way toward the banks of the creek, keeping close to the rock on the lower side, till he arrives a little outward from the current where the waters formd an eddy, as denoted by a mixture of alluvium with the sand and gravel of the creek. In those situations, he may expect to find gold. If he finds gold in such a locality, he may prospect outward toward the banks of the creek, till he has exhausted the whole deposit.

As the tilted rocks of the gold district have universally one course, and as creeks meander across them in nearly every possible direction, there are chances in many places for reefs of rocks to traverse the beds of creeks, directly along their channels. Under such circumstances, but little gold has been deposited. If the miner continues his search along the creek downward, till he arrives at a bend in it, where the water is forcd over such reefs, a little outward from the channel, gold is often found in great abundance— watching carefully whilst excavating the earth in such places, to prospect the lower side of any reefs that may be found there.

If a rock of several feet in hight traverse crosswise the whole width of a creek, so that the only passage for the water of the stream is over it, like the fall of a mill-dam, its force seldom allows gold to be deposited near to it. But a short distance below, where the first quiet waters occurd, gold may be found in lateral and central pockets and little basin-shapd hollows of the rock at the bottom of creek deposits.

Again, if a rock project from any portion of the stream, so high that water cannot run over it but is forcd around it, an eddy is in such case formd immediately below it, in which situation gold may be expected to be found.

In some situations, along some of the creeks, as at Sullivan's camp, on one of the tributaries of the St. Waukeen, the slate rock, on which the gold was deposited, has since been decomposd to a considerable depth below the tertiary deposit. It would seem that a second solubility of the iron deposits had taken place, and liberated the gold to settle down into the decomposd rock. In such situations, the miner continues to prospect downward, as long as he finds gold abundant enough to reward his labors.

Creek-washd gold is sometimes found higher up in the banks from the current of creeks than the experiencd miner is aware of, but the man acquainted with the appearance of creek-worn pebbles is never at a loss to determine the agent that placd them there—and if, in such situations, he finds rounded, creek worn pebbles, he may conclude that the pebbles and gold also were deposited there by water. In such cases, it becomes the miner to examine the bearing and level of the creek above such place, and see if the creek may not some day have formd an eddy there, and deposited its various contents. If, still higher up in the bank, he finds gold entirely angular, he may conclude that it has slidden down from the hill above.

Another thing to be observd by the miner, relative to creek-gold, is, that in prospecting up and down creeks for gold,—he carefully observe where a level expanse is formd at the foot of a cascade. Near the head of such expanse, between the cascade above, and the next one below, he will find gold more abundant than toward the lower end of such expanse.

In searching for eddies of creeks, where the greatest amount of gold is often deposited, the miner should bear in mind that eddies formd in time of freshets, are most likely to contain the most and heaviest gold, from the fact that much power is requird to move heavy gold, and tertiary sediment.

Mode of searching for the Third Variety

To obtain a knowledge of prospecting for bar gold, requires also a knowledge of the philosophy of running waters—yet gold is prospected with less difficulty in the bars of large rivers than creek-gold.

As the bar gold is very light and thin, it is subject to the various freaks of running water, in which it is mechanically suspended, during times of freshets. In prospecting therefore, for gold along the bars of rivers, the principal thing to be attended to, is the formation of eddies along those streams, which, if the edges of the water were straight and unbroken, through the length of a bar, would also be formd along in straight lines but a short distance from shore, or outer edge of the water. These eddies are the intermediate line between the downward current of the stream, and the retrograde or upward movement of the water along the shore, where water is nearly in a quiescent state.

But as the edges of streams are rough and uneven, the eddies are also formd uneven. Hence, a deposit of gold in those eddies, is not straight, but varies according to the unevenness of the shore.

Such a line of quiet water, is the only deposit of bar gold which is likely to be richest, near the heads of bars.

The best method of prospecting for bar gold, is to commence an excavation, a short distance out from the water of the river, near the head of a bar, digging downward but a short distance among the sand and gravel, occasionally washing the earth.—And if gold is found, progress toward and from the river, till the richest deposit is found. Then change the course upward and downward the river, and continue to prospect as long as gold is abundant enough to pay for working.

As this gold is subject to subsequent removals by every succeeding freshet, it never gets deeply embedded in any solid tertiary deposits. Hence, it is most usually found among loose sand and gravel, near the surface.

This search should be made when the water of rivers is quite low, which time is also best in searching for the other two varieties.

If along a line of bar deposit, a rock is found protruding high—gold may be expected more abundant immediately below it, than elsewhere.

To those searching for gold along the bars of rivers, it was at first, not a little surprising to learn that but little gold was deposited toward the center of the stream—but on reflection,—it will be seen that the water is too violent to admit floating gold to come to rest in such situations.

CHAPTER XXII

Cost of transporting Goods from the several embarkadaries to the mines—Price of Merchandize in the mines—Cost of Provisions—Price of Medical Services—Administration of Justice—Manner of spending the Sabbath.

From the two principal embarkadaries upon the St. Waukeen and Sacramento rivers of California, provisions and mining implements are transported to the seat of mining operations at exorbitant costs.

On passing up to the mines from a place calld Stocton, upon the St. Waukeen, our company hird a teamster to carry our goods and implements, for which we paid him, for one wagon load, more than *fourteen hundred dollars*, rated at 30 cents per pound. Afterwards during the summer, goods were carrid on pack mules at a somewhat less cost. It may also be added, that conveyances were got up for the accommodation of passengers between Stocton and the mines, a distance of 70 or 80 miles, at a charge of 2 ounces of gold dust for each passenger, which, according to its value in California, is worth $32.

From Sacramento city, the present head of navigation upon the Sacramento river, similar prices are chargd for the transportation of goods into that quarter of the mining district.

The price of merchandize at the mines is quite dissimilar to prices in the States. Tea, best, per pound, is worth from $2 to $4. Common sizd frying pans at $8. Tin pans, a large size, at $8 apiece. India rubber elastic cots at $50 to $75 each. Calf-skin shoes, per pair, at $8, and boots at $16. An ordinary article of ax-helve at $3. Lumber, scarce, at $2 per ft. Pint tin cups at $1.50 each. Coarse sheeting, 50 cents per yard.

The cost of provisions ranges somewhat as follows. Flour is worth, per pound, from 75 cts. to $1. Pork, per pound, $1. Beans are sold by the pound, at $1 per pound. Rice, per lb., 62½ cents. Light bread, per loaf of one pound, $1. Beef, 25 cents the pound. Potatoes are sold by the pound, at 50 cents. Green peas preservd in air-tight jars, per pint, $4. Onions, per pound, $2. Public meals, $2.

Medical services are likewise high, in the mining district. Each visit, near to patient, is 1 oz. of gold, or $16. If a week's attendance is requird, no reduction upon each visit is made. For extracting a tooth, $10 is chargd. Very extravagant prices are chargd for distant visits.

In relation to the *administration of justice* in the mining district, wherever a sufficient assemblage of miners exists to be thought worthy of judicial attention, an alcalda or justice of the peace is appointed, who presides over the judiciary department, with almost as unlimited sway as an emperor. And although in addition to an alcalda, a sheriff is appointed to a permanent office, and cases are almost universally tried by a jury, which is summond by the sheriff, yet they are generally selected of a stamp congruous to the feelings of the alcalda. From the decisions, no appeal can ever be made, whether right or wrong. I would likewise remark, that decisions are very apt to be made against the party having the most gold, and especially if one of the parties is rather low in circumstances. Such a state of judicial dispensation may seem somewhat objectionable, at first thought, but when we reflect, that where no legislation exists, lynch law is the only mode of dispensing justice, to which men can well resort, and this is so terrific in its consequences of criminal justice, that rogues tremble in view of its administration. Much more civility and less theft exists in the mines than might at first be supposd.

The costs of legal services may be arrangd somewhat as follows: Alcaldas, for each suit, 1 oz. To the sheriff, 1 oz. To each juryman, half an ounce of gold,—and legal pleadings are often enormous, even to $100 for the service of an hour or two.

The several foregoing costs of transportation, price of merchandize, costs of provisions and medical services, are very often increasd or diminishd, according to location, distance, or difficulty of transporting, and also the season of the year.

There is a consideration, likewise, in relation to *spending the Sabbath amongst the gold mines of California.*

The reader may greatly wonder what is the mode of spending the Sabbath there, when I say to him, that the Sabbath appears as silent as the house of mourning. Seldom is a man seen with his implements in his hands, laboring for gold. All around is quiet, except now and then a few horsemen are passing from one little town to another, for purposes best known to themselves. What, then, is the wonderful employment or idle condition of miners upon that day? Alas! every public tent through the whole mining region is resorted to for gambling. In each of these tents, stands from one to four or six monte tables, around which, miners of all classes assemble to risk their fortunes. These tables are arrangd with small or large sums of money, by one or more persons, according to the ability of the person or persons that establish them. The sums of money so arrangd are calld banks, or monte banks. On opposite sides of the table, sit two men, who manage the affairs of the bank, and deal the cards by which the fate of bettors is determind. This game at cards is carrid on from morning till night, and often through the following night till twilight breaks upon them, with the stillness and quiet of a religious assemblage.

DESCRIPTION OF CALIFORNIA

CHAPTER XXIII

Alta or Upper California With respect to Agriculture—
Climate and Health of Alta California—Navigation of its
two principal Rivers—Some of the principal Towns of Alta
California—Its Bays and Harbors.

It can hardly be imagind, how the business of agriculture can be carrid on successfully in a country circumstancd like Upper California. In the mountainous portions, grain can not do well without resort to irrigation, and this, from extreme cost, can not well be done on an extensive scale.

The low country of the great valley of the St. Waukeen and Sacramento, is not unfrequently inundated a month or two, during the latter part of the winter, which renders passages from one part of the valley to another by land, entirely impracticable, and although along the borders of those two large rivers, and to some distance outward from them, there is a good soil, yet it is well known to farmers, that wheat will not live but a few days, entirely immersd in water—so that the wheat crop could never be depended upon as a safe investment.

Along the borders of these rivers, in some places, the native grasses are of a tolerable growth. Outward toward the base of the mountain, the earth becomes so dry during the summer, that vegetation is entirely dried up. It however arrives at maturity, at a stinted growth. I have seen native oats growing upon the plains of the great valley. These also are not very enormous in size. Notwithstanding, they for awhile furnish good grazing for the roaming cattle of the country, upon which, and the short bunch grass growing upon some of the hills, they become very fat during the summer. But as the grasses of the country are of so stinted a growth, farmers cannot live in crowded communities, as in the States, but at distances of from 10 to 20 miles apart. Locations of this kind are calld ranches, or rancheros, and farmers so living often own several hundred head of cattle and horses.

The climate of California, of which I shall next speak, varies considerably in different parts of the country, according to its distance from the ocean or from the Neveda mountains, or the unevenness of the surface of the country.

In the mountain district of the Neveda range, the climate was describd in the geography of that portion of California.

Lower down and westward, along the great valley, the climate is milder, through the whole of the year. I believe the large rivers of the valley are not frozen during the winter, and the weather in summer is quite warm. Thus far from the axis of the Neveda mountains eastward, to the two great rivers westward, during the summer season, the sky is serene, and the stars and planets shine with great splendor.

No dew falls in that part hitherto describd, during the hottest season of the year, and travelers may lie upon the ground without exposure from the unhealthiness of a damp ground and a moist atmosphere.

Farther outward, and along the coast, the country is much of the time during the year, coverd with fogs, which render it unpleasant, and in some measure unhealthy. The town of San Francisco, most of the year, is envelopd in a thick fog, during much of the night and the following day, till 10 or 11 o'clock, after which time the wind becomes of sufficient strength to clear away the fog, which often renders the remainder of the day unpleasant. This town, from the almost continued dampness of the atmosphere, and the unavoidable use of mineralizd water, can hardly be considerd a healthy place. Dysentery and fever seems to be the prevalent disease.

I had nearly forgotten an idea which I now recollect to have heard, relating to the dryness and purity of the atmosphere of California. It has been said that the flesh of animals may be hung up in the open atmosphere, till it becomes perfectly preservd by drying, without salt, and during such process, no annoying insects ever disturb it—and also, that a man would never die there, except by being dried up.

It is true, that the Spaniards have a mode of preserving the flesh of the ox, by cutting it into very small strips, and hanging it upon strings cut from the raw hide, where it is exposd to the heat of the sun. In this way, meat could be preservd in any of the States, but if it be left in large masses, and so circumstancd that any part of it is kept from drying immediately on the outside, the green fly, an insect common to that country as well as the States, is presently found to be a loathsome intruder.

When I left the mining district for the valley, on my way to San Francisco, on the 13th of October, I saw eight or ten vessels lying at Stocton, and at the head of Suisan bay, three or four more, and at the head of Pablo bay, six or seven more. These, with ten or twelve lying at Sacramento city, and as many more scatterd along the two rivers and in the several bays, added to about 130 which I counted in the harbor of San Francisco, on my arrival there, will make about 175 vessels within the country of California. Most of the vessels lying in the harbor of San Francisco, were inactive, for want of help to work them.

The business of transportation upon the two rivers, St. Waukeen and Sacramento, I believe to be as profitable as any that is attended to in California. When I left, two small steamers were constantly plying between San Francisco and Sacramento city, and another was being put together at Suisan bay, for the navigation of the St. Waukeen. More busines at present is done upon the rivers by launches, a small vessel of only one mast, than by any other vessel. These are more easily managd than large ships, along the intricate windings of those extremely crooked rivers, but so soon as a sufficient number of steamers can be obtaind for the business of the rivers, other means of transportation will in a great degree cease.

That portion of Alta California, where at present men's conceptions are most vivid, and where at every corner, pass or avenue, the lively turn of the foot is seen, and where men's views and feelings to-morrow will not be what they are to-day, and where also the sight of the golden streams from the Neveda mountains produce electrical shocks upon all persons, whose hearts are tund to chant the new and animating lays of later scenes of better days, and where nearly all of the "Elephant," in his varied and portentous displays, is seen—may be comprisd within the small tract of country, over which the waters of the two principal rivers, Sacramento and St. Waukeen, flow. Along these waters, are several newly laid out towns, together with some of ancient Mexican date.

San Francisco is situated upon a side hill, on the south side of the bay of the same name. Its inhabitants were reckond, on the first of November, '49, at 25,000, though six months before there were scarcely 5000. Such has been the rapid progress of San Francisco. The town is 10 or 12 miles within the entrance of the bay from the ocean.

At the head of Pablo bay, is a newly laid out town, calld Benetia. It lies on the north side of the strait between Pablo bay and Suisan bay. This strait will doubtless bear the name of Benetia. The town will ultimately be a pleasanter one than San Francisco. One mile east of Benetia, upon the same side of the strait, the United States have establishd an arsenal.

At the head of Suisan bay, is a new town calld Western New York. This town lies on the south side of the waters of the bay, upon, a flat piece of ground, at the lower confluence of the Sacramento and St. Waukeen. The delta between the upper and lower confluence, is about 20 miles in length. New York, situated as it is, will command the business of both rivers, and if it is lucky enough to avoid being inundated once a year, will ultimately be a place of considerable importance.

At the present head waters of navigation for the St. Waukeen, upon a slough about three miles distant from the river, is a town calld Stocton, the principal embarkadary for the south division of the mining district. This town is situated on low, flat ground, which rises but little above the waters of the river, at lowest stages. When the country around is overflowd with water, this town must necessarily suffer much inconvenience therefrom.

The last town which I shall here mention, is Sacramento city. Like Stocton, it is situated at the present head waters of the Sacramento river. It serves as the principal embarkadary for the northern mining region, as Stocton does for the south, and from this place, provisions and implements are carrid to all parts of the northern mining region. The place is more than half as large as San Francisco, and is fast improving.

Before closing the subject of California, a few remarks concerning its *bays and harbors* may not be uninteresting.

The Bay of San Francisco is nearly surrounded by high hills, with a narrow entrance from the ocean, and now and then an island is interspersd, to hide the scenery of its waters from the hills contiguous to the town of San Francisco. It is large enough to contain the shipping of the whole world, and its waters are not of inconvenient depth for anchorage.

Next above this, lies Pablo bay, or Bay of St. Paul. It is inferior in size, but ships can anchor in any part of it, and lie at all times with a tolerable degree of safety.

At the head of Pablo bay, commences Suisan bay, which extends upward to the delta that divides the two rivers, Sacramento and St. Waukeen. The waters of this bay are so shoal that vessels have difficulty in sailing over it, except directly along its channel.

The distances across the several bays are as follows. From San Francisco to Pablo bay, is about 10 miles, and through Pablo bay to Suisan bay, is 40 miles, and Suisan bay differs but little from 50 miles in length, from Benetia to New York, at the head of the bay.

HOMEWARD BOUND

CHAPTER XXIV

Scenes on the Pacific Ocean.—Difficulty of reaching the harbor of Panama, by sail ships.—Arrival at Panama.—The town of Panama, and its inhabitants.—Passage across the isthmus, to Chagres.

After a stay in California of a little more than five months, I took my departure for home by way of the ocean, on board a sail ship bound for Panama, the 21st day of October, 1849. As there is often a difficulty in getting out of the bay of San Francisco into the ocean, with sail ships, on account of a strong wind that is much of the time blowing through the straits eastward from the ocean, and the dense fog that envelops the sea, at the entrance of the bay, we were detaind nearly two days before we could pass the straits into the ocean.

Our passage from San Francisco to Panama, was accomplishd in 40 days, a distance of about 4000 miles, tho' along the coast, it would not much exceed 3500. This passage was considerd by the master of the vessel, as expeditious as is common upon waters of as little wind as is not unfrequently witnessd upon the Pacific ocean.

Whilst on my passage from Oregon last spring, to California, I saw a short distance from ship, a whale, in an attempt at running a race with us. He kept along in a parallel course with the ship, one or two miles, and then left us. Ship-masters say they will outrun the fleetest ship.

But we saw on our passage from San Francisco to Panama, but few of the monsters of the deep, so often describd in history and romance, although this coast is the place to which whalemen resort. At a distance from ship, we saw now and then a few whales, spouting the briny waters high into the atmosphere—and then again, a shoal of porpoises surrounding the ship— some of which, our sailors caught with their hooks and lines.—The flesh of the porpoise is of a reddish color, and coarse, but tolerably pleasant to eat.

The dolphin is a small fish of only two or three feet in length—and has the power of changing its color. The flesh is said to be poisonous in some degree, and is therefore not good for food. These fish are shy and hard to take, except by stratagem.

Our captain is an old whaleman, and his vessel was fitted out from Nantucket, for that purpose. On our way south,—he one day took 4 or 5 men into a whale-boat, and started out from the vessel in pursuit of some black fish we saw at a short distance from us. We had not watchd him long before we saw him returning with a large black fish in tow of his whale boat. He presently came along side, and down the halyards were let—to haul the monster upon deck,—and in a few minutes, was seen stretchd athwart the ship, a giant fish, weighing about 2500 pounds,—out of which, was obtain 4 barrels of oil.

This was a specimen of whaling on a small scale. The fish here caught, was a species of whale, and was organizd similarly. A few inches from the end of his snout, upon the top of it, was a valve, about 3 inches square, out of which, the animal spouts.

After tossing and rolling about upon the wide Pacific, till I was utterly tird of my situation, we at length arrivd at the outer confines of Panama bay, on Monday, Nov. 26. Although this bay is more than 100 miles wide at the entrance, yet it is so situated, that most of the year, there is a wind from the Caribbean sea, blowing across the continent outward from the harbor of Panama, which renders an entrance into it slow and difficult. We, however, after tacking the ship the tedious number of 10 times, arrivd in safety at the harbor of Panama, on the evening of Friday, Nov. 30.

Our arrival at Panama, was an epoch of satisfaction to me, as well as my fellow passengers, after having experienced so many days of monotony upon the ocean.

The anchorage for ships is inconveniently situated from town, being nearly 3 miles distant.

After having arrivd at the town, and wanderd over it somewhat, I found it to be located upon a rock, formd of successive layers of apparent lava. But as my opportunity of examining it was scanty, I could not well determine its character. The town wears a dilapidated appearance, from its extreme age, and a want of attention to repairs. Many of the houses are large,—and three stories high, with broken down roofs, and with grass growing out of every corner, and upon the roofs. They have the oddity of being built partly of bricks, and partly of stone, intermingld together in the body of the walls. They have windows arrangd similar to windows in houses of the states, but without sash or glass, being left entirely open. No chimneys are built to any of the houses, and cooking is done with small portable furnaces, or a fire is built upon the ground, between 2 small rocks set up edgewise, so as to contain the fuel. In the cooking apartments, an arrangement is made for the escape of the smoke at the top of the room, so that it may not communicate with their dining or sitting rooms.

The town, previous to the gold excitement of California, was in a great measure, vacant of inhabitants, and large and commodious rooms may have been hird for the small sum of 12½ cents per day. The streets are mostly narrow, but they are tolerably well pavd, and are washd nearly every day for ¾ of a year, from the all copious fountain of the heavens above. No drays or coaches are seen to mar the beauty of the streets, and grass is seen growing even in the middle of the streets, and along its sidewalks. This was once a populous town, but now—like most other Spanish towns along the western coast of America, is seen the marks of imbecility, indifference and decay. They have a small market or two, to which all classes indiscriminately, resort for their daily support. The town next to the bay is walld around, upon which, a few cannon were placd for its former defense.

The inhabitants speak the Spanish language. They are cleanly in dress, plain in their manners, and familiar in their conversation. They are unassuming in their style, and liberal in their hospitalities.

I am inclind to think the character of the American Spanish has hitherto been misrepresented. During my stay in California, I was located among that people, and I ever found them willing to part with half their last meal to feed a hungry man. Although the Spanish ladies are almost universally neat washers, yet their is a want of taste in their dress, it being loosely, though not fantastically adjusted about their persons. In their behavior, their sitting and reclining postures have an unchaste appearance, though this may arise from want of proper training.

The width of the isthmus from Panama across to the bay of Darien, is not much different from 50 miles—but by the way of the old Panama road to Chagres, the distance is about 64 miles. Through this route the present emigration passes.—From Panama, there is a portage of about 24 miles, to Cruses, a town of about 150 houses, at the present head waters of the Chagres river. There is also, another town of similar importance, about 5 miles below, upon the Chagres river, calld Gorgona. To this town, also, there is a road which leads off from the Cruses road about half way distant from Panama to Cruses.

The present Cruses road is probably of as ancient date as the town of Panama. It has once been pavd, and a tolerably good road for pack animals to pass, but too narrow to admit of carriages. Across the portage, the country is uneven, though not mountainous, and much of the way, the road is cut through hills of soft rock. At present, the pavement is almost all broken up, and the road is muddy and disagreeable to pass, much of the year, even with pack animals. Most of the property that now passes that road, is carrid upon the backs of native citizens,—though horses or mules can be hird at either end of the rout for the transportation of property.

The houses of Cruses and Gorgona, and also a few scattering houses along the portage, are made of Bamboo, a reed which grows very tall, but small in size. These reeds are set upon the ends, and firmly crowded together to the size of the requird wall. At the corners of these walls, are set posts of sufficient strength to support the roofs, which are thatchd of the cocoa leaf. After the roofs are completed, no rains can penetrate them. The slender appearance of these houses, seems to be a proof that no tornados or heavy winds exist along the isthmus,—and some families live in tenements of nothing but a roof placd upon posts in the form of a Dutch barrack.

The remainder of the way from Cruses to Chagres, is down the Chagres river,—a stream of considerable importance in time of high water, though not of sufficient depth to admit of the navigation of any but small class steamboats, in times of common stages of the river.

The country across the isthmus truly indicates a want of yankee enterprise. No agricultural interests are resorted to for the support of the inhabitants. All appears drear, and the country is thickly coverd with low, leafy kinds of timber, heavily laden much of it, with vines of various kinds, pending their branches near to the ground. Now and then, however, along the way is seen a small opening or lawn, where a few cattle are grazing— and these of the thriftiest kind,—indicating the advantages which might be derivd from the improvement of the soil upon the isthmus.

CHAPTER XXV

Town of Chagres—Its inhabitants—Trip to New Orleans—
Thence up the Mississippi to St. Louis—Arrival home.

Chagres is a town of some over 150 houses, situated on the South American side, at the mouth of the Chagres river. The houses are like those of Gorgona and Cruses, many of which appear to be of considerably ancient date. The ground upon which the town stands, is of but little elevation above the waters of the river, and it seems that it must inevitably become inundated, should a strong wind continue to blow a considerable time from off the Caribbean sea. This town, as also Gorgona, Cruses and Panama, belongs to the republic of New Grenada. Bogota is the capital of this republic, and is situated interior, several hundred miles to the south of Chagres. An entrance to the mouth of the Chagres river, by sail ships, is often attended with the danger of being wreckd on the beach. Hence, a steamer is kept at the harbor for the conveyance of passengers from them, at a distance of 2 miles, where they are obligd to anchor.

At the entrance of the river and contiguous to the town, upon a projecting eminence, is an old, dilapidated fort, with a large number of brass cannon scatterd about upon the walls. There appear to be a few soldiers strolling about the fort, but with a total indifference to the attention which a fort requires for its requisite abilities, in an emergency.

The inhabitants of Chagres have more of negroes and negro blood in them than the citizens of Panama, Cruses or Gorgona, but they are of similar stamp with their neighbors in that part of America, and speak the same language. The females dress much in lawns and other light clothing, as is most suitable for the climate. The religion here, and mostly throughout this part of the country, is Roman Catholic.

The bells of the churches are generally hung in the windows, or outside, near the ground, at their entrances. The cross-bar on which they are hung, often contains two bells, so that the ringing of them is frequently done by two persons, in quite a ludicrous manner. The mode of ringing is performd by each person's taking a small hammer or stick, and striking upon the outside of the bells, keeping time with each other, similar to the beating of two drummers.

Saturday, Dec. 8th.—Embarkd on board brig Major Eastland, bound to New Orleans, and arrivd there, Thursday, December 20th. Our trip was a tolerably short and pleasant one, for the season of the year. We experiencd no storm upon the Caribbean sea, nor any through the Gulf of Mexico. Nothing of importance was experiencd on the way, to change the monotony.

On the 21st, I left New Orleans by steamboat, for St Louis, a distance of 1200 miles by water, though probably not much exceeding 600 direct. The old towns of Natchez and Vicksburg are in a decayd condition. Memphis appears to be the most thriving town between New Orleans and St. Louis.

Monday, Dec. 31st, I found myself at the St. Louis levee, after struggling with floating ice for a day or two, the latter part of the distance. I left St. Louis, Jan. 2d, 1850, and arrivd at Knox co., Ill., Jan. 8th, having been gone from home, one year, nine months and five days.

On my arrival at home, I found my friends in a state of health, though many deaths in town had occurd during my absence, and the place had exceedingly improvd.

A few remarks appendant to the foregoing, in relation to traveling expenses, may be of use to those desirous to go to California, by the way of the oceans and the isthmus. At present, the arrangement for running steamers between San Francisco and Panama, is, to leave each place for the other, but twice each month, which is on the 1st and 20th. Sail ships are also running between the two places with frequency. Prices of passage, the fall of 1849, between the two places, were $300 cabin, $150 steerage. On board sail ships, $150 cabin, and $75 steerage. An arrangement from Chagres to New York, by the way of New Orleans and Havana, is made by the U. S. Mail Ship Company, for carrying passengers, so that passengers can leave Chagres on the 28th of each month, at $150 cabin, $125 forward, and $80 steerage. This state of things will not last long, before there will be a sufficient amount of competition for the speedy accommodation of all who wish to go to California.

9 789362 768018